MW01286080

Trading
NATURAL GAS

**Cash
Futures
Options
and
Swaps**

Trading
NATURAL GAS

Cash
Futures
Options
and
Swaps

Fletcher J. Sturm

Copyright© 1997 by
PennWell Corporation
1421 South Sheridan Road
Tulsa, Oklahoma 74112-6000 USA

800-752-9764
+1-918-831-9421
sales@pennwell.com
www.pennwell.com
www.pennwellbooks.com

Director: Mary McGee
Production / Operations Manager: Traci Huntsman
Senior Design Editor: Robin Remaley

Library of Congress Cataloging-in-Publication Data
Sturm, Fletcher H.
  Trading natural gas : cash futures options and swaps / by Fletcher J. Sturm
  p. cm.
  Includes index.
  ISBN 0-87814-709-8
  ISBN13 978-0-87814-709-0
  1. Gas industry–Finance 2. Commodity exchanges. 3. Futures market.
4. Options (Finance) 5. Swaps (Finance) I. Title
HG6047.N37S78 1996
332.64'42285–dc21   96-51043
                              CIP

Printed in the United States of America

10

Table of Contents

Preface

The thought of writing this book came to me in the same way a trader recognizes a trading opportunity: supply and demand. During my time in the natural gas industry, I have frequently encountered individuals and companies looking for publications that explain the dynamics of the industry as well as the numerous hedging and trading instruments being used. Aside from in-house manuals and presentation material provided by industry leaders, there is a paucity of information available to the general public that provides introductory material on the industry itself or information on more advanced topics such as natural gas derivative trading instruments. As a result, I realized that such a book on this market is in high demand and short supply. This book is my effort to fill the void. It covers a wide variety of subjects, some in more detail than others, but it is generally intended for newcomers to the natural gas market, or those who want to learn more about particular market segments (e.g., physical, futures, and other derivatives).

Chapter 1, "Overview," provides a brief overview of the evolution of the market from the over-regulated business it once was, into what it is today. Discussion in this section is limited to the main topics and turning points that moved the natural gas market to deregulation, excluding some of the repercussions of deregulation such as "take-or-pay" issues.

Chapter 2, "The Physical (Cash) Natural Gas Market," offers a fundamental picture of the market as it exists today, including supply and demand forces, transportation and storage, and natural gas trading rituals.

Chapter 3, "The Financial Natural Gas Market," outlines the concepts of the utilitarian value and the monetary value of natural gas. In addition, a basic overview of transaction pricing structure is covered.

Chapter 4, "Hedging and Trading Instruments," covers all types of trading products used in the natural gas market, defined and demonstrated through examples of typical trades and other applications.

Chapter 5, "Structured Transactions," is a series of examples of more complex trades common among market participants.

Chapter 6, "Building a Risk Management Model," offers a framework for developing various business units within a trading group which orbit the risk management function.

I hope this book is informative, enjoyable, and that it inspires newcomers to the natural gas industry, as well as veterans, to learn more about trading natural gas and to become better natural gas traders.

List of Figures and Captions

Chapter 1

Introduction

The natural gas industry is a dynamic, complex, and exciting place to be at the *current* time. Employing more than a million people in North America alone, the market continues to grow due to ever-increasing opportunities from exploration and production, to marketing and trading, to transportation and consumption. Although most widely used in North America, natural gas consumption is spreading throughout the world. Many emerging countries and even more advanced industrialized nations are diversifying their energy consumption by encouraging the exploration for natural gas and the development of transmission systems to distribute natural gas throughout their countries for its many uses.

This chapter provides the reader with a general understanding of the evolution of the natural gas market from its early regulated environment to the current stage of the industry. I will refer the reader to other sources for information pertaining to the discovery of natural gas, production methodologies, legal issues stemming from deregulation, and other topics not related to the subsequent material in this book.

Industry Segments

In the United States, the natural gas industry was originally comprised of two segments: exploration and production and distribution and sales. Initially, the exploration and production segment was not viewed as a part of the industry in need of regulation but as a natural resource extraction industry. The distribution and sales segment, however, was controlled exclusively by the major natural gas pipeline companies and was viewed as a business in need of regulation primarily because transmission of the product by these pipelines served the public interest most effectively and efficiently. Due to the high cost of entry to the market, geographical limitations, and environmental feasibility, local governments felt a monopolistic threat could develop among these few transmission companies. Consequently, local governments declared authority over the geographic areas containing natural gas pipelines.

As the natural gas market continued to grow, pipelines began to spread from one geographic region to another, crossing state borders and hence local government jurisdictions. The rules governing one state differed from those in others and it became apparent that regulation of the industry should be administered by a federal government agency. Interstate natural gas pipelines were deemed public utilities by the federal government, establishing the right of eminent domain, and pipeline owners were therefore required to conduct their business in a way which served the public interest.

Natural Gas Act of 1938

Exercising its right under the U. S. Constitution, Congress passed the Natural Gas Act (NGA) of 1938 in order to implement the principles and regulations which would protect the public interest. To implement these principles, the NGA created the Federal Power Commission (FPC) as the administrative agency responsible for overseeing this objective. The guiding principles under the Natural Gas Act of 1938 are still inherent in some regulations in place today, and they continue to be leading factors in proposed rule making changes.

The most important regulatory development under the NGA was found in section 7(c), which required pipelines to obtain certification prior to building transmission lines, abandoning old lines not in use, or providing transmission services at approved transmission rates. Approval to build natural gas pipelines was, and still is, required in order to ensure that the need for the pipeline exists, and that its purpose would serve the public interest. In addition, the cost of building these transmission systems had to be viewed as a prudent cost. An old transmission line could only be abandoned if it was of little or no use to the public due to changing market characteristics. Approved transmission rates were established that would allow costs prudently incurred by the pipelines from conducting its business in a manner which served the public interest to be fully recovered in addition to earning a reasonable rate of return on assets. These approval documents became commonly known as 7(c) certificates. The FPC was mandated to establish these parameters and rely on the courts to confirm or overturn them. The process worked well until market forces changed the dynamics of the industry and set the stage for more adaptive change.

The Phillips Decision

The natural gas market enjoyed a period of substantial growth during the 1940s and 1950s as industrial business demand for natural gas accelerated due to World War II. During this time however, supply and demand discrepancies began to emerge in various geographic regions due to limited pipeline accessibility and regulated transmission rates. Natural gas prices fluctuated wildly, and as a result, the FPC was encouraged by natural gas producers to establish price controls over the exploration and production (E & P) segment. The FPC resisted, however, by claiming that the NGA did not give it the authority to do so and that it was not in the public interest. The courts did not agree with this logic, and in the Phillips decision (1954) the U.S. Supreme Court ordered the FPC to establish control over prices to be paid to natural gas producers at the wellhead (production site). Additionally, the FPC was ordered to include the E & P segment under the section 7(c) certification

2

process. The court based its ruling on the premise that it was not possible to control the sales price charged to consumers by the pipeline companies if the pipeline owners could not control the procurement costs. As such, it was determined that this did not protect the public interest. The effect of this ruling shifted the dynamics of the market in a way which began setting the stage for the eventual deregulation of both the E & P and the sales and distribution segments of the natural gas market.

Effects of Phillips Decision

The outcome of the Phillips decision essentially allowed for the exploration and production segment to receive a predetermined "cap" or maximum price for its supply into the interstate natural gas pipeline systems. As a result, with limited upside profit potential and rising exploration and production costs, natural gas producers began looking for alternative markets for their supply.

While the overall market for natural gas was surging during this time, the non-regulated intrastate market was outpacing the overall rate of growth of the market. (An *intrastate pipeline* is operated and physically located within the same state, as opposed to an *interstate pipeline* which spans two or more states.) This shift in growth was happening for two reasons. First, and most importantly, wellhead prices into intrastate pipelines were not regulated by the FPC, but came under the jurisdiction of the local governing body in that particular geographic region, usually the state. And because local governments did not have the authority to set price controls, the price of natural gas was free to fluctuate according to what the market would bear. The market was tight due to increased demand, and, consequently, prices into the intrastate pipelines returned a higher wellhead profit to the producers. Second, producers were saving administrative expenses when selling into the intrastate pipelines by avoiding expenses pertaining to the filing for section 7(c) certificates. (The filing and approval process with the FPC was taking from 6 to 18 months.) Ultimately, in the 1970s, supply shortages developed on most major interstate pipelines serving the large market areas, thus threatening the stability of the interstate natural gas industry.

Natural Gas Policy Act of 1978

In 1978, Congress reversed the Phillips decision with the passage of the Natural Gas Policy Act (NGPA) which reformed wellhead natural gas price controls and outlined the need to restructure the distribution and sales segment through "open-access" to the market areas. The NGPA established the Federal Energy Regulatory Commission (FERC) in order to administer and achieve the objectives of the policy act. The goals of the NGPA were to increase supply on the interstate pipelines through reform of wellhead price controls and to foster a more competitive environment in the consuming regions (market areas) along the interstate pipeline systems.

To achieve the first goal, the FERC designed and established a preset formula which allowed wellhead prices to rise. This effectively subsidized natural gas prices by increasing the cost paid by end-users. As a result of the "pent-up" demand, prices rose and continued to rise by the amount allowed under the preset formula set by the FERC. Producers were able to immediately increase production and, as they were capable of projecting further price increases according to the formula set by the FERC, they dramatically accelerated additional drilling ventures. From 1979 through the early 1980s more than 4,000 natural gas drilling rigs were operating in the United States, compared with approximately 450 operating in 1996. This production boom clearly showed that the FERC was successful in achieving its first goal of stimulating supply to meet demand. However, the second goal, improving the demand side of the equation, proved to be more elusive.

As unforeseen jurisdictional and bureaucratic problems surfaced, open-access to the marketplace never materialized. The principal issue was how to restructure the services provided by the pipelines and distribution companies in order to increase market competitiveness. This issue would not be resolved until nearly 10 years later.

Business in the E & P segment, on the other hand, could not have been better as the production surge continued until the market became heavily oversupplied. As my grandfather used to say in good times and bad, "This too will pass!" Eventually, the gas boom of the 1980s did pass as prices began to collapse.

Orders 436 and 500

The most constructive effort led by market participants and the FERC to further deregulate and revitalize the natural gas industry emerged in the format of the FERC Open Access Rule Orders 436 and 500. The concept of Orders 436 and 500 was to allow pipelines to continue buying gas from producers and selling to end users in the traditional manner, but to also allow producers and end users to enter into contracts with the pipelines to obtain capacity on these transmission systems for their own use. The logic was that producers could then sell directly to end users and end users could buy directly from producers, utilizing their own capacity on the pipelines to "ship" the supply from the production areas to the market areas themselves. In addition, to cope with the anticipated administrative burden of how to specify *when* and *how much* gas to receive and deliver, as well as how to identify which gas volumes belonged to which party, orders 436 and 500 also set forth certain procedures for nominating (reserving capacity) and allocating (segregating and measuring) the natural gas volumes being shipped. (These procedures worked well until differences between volumes received and volumes delivered occurred. This situation is known as a pipeline imbalance, and is resolved through imbalance penalties imposed by the pipelines if not corrected within a specified grace period.) Furthermore, orders 436 and 500 led to the development of various transportation tariff structures by the pipelines, which identify different levels of transportation service. As a result, shippers (title holders which transport natural gas on a pipeline) could choose between more or less reliable transportation service, as well as transportation service for varying lengths of time, depending on how much they were willing to pay for that service. For example, transportation service for one month which could be interrupted at the pipeline's discretion (interruptible service) would be less expensive than transportation service for one year which could not be interrupted by the pipeline (firm service).

Mega-NOPR

The next step to achieving a more open market environment came on July 31, 1991 when the FERC issued a Notice of Proposed Rule-making (NOPR) which opened discussions on the way pipelines should restructure their service arrangements in a way which would conform to the changing industry structure and maintain competitiveness. The phrase "Mega-NOPR" was coined in anticipation of the impact on the industry from the restructuring, and after a lengthy comment and review process, the Mega-NOPR became FERC Final Order 636—The Restructuring Rule, issued on April 9, 1992.

The Final Order 636 brought together the open-access concepts in Orders 436 and 500 and, in general, outlined the "unbundling" of services provided by the interstate pipelines. *Unbundling* is the process of identifying and separating the various services provided by a pipeline and allowing these services to be contracted for, independent of one another. *Bundling*, on the other hand, is the term used for "rolling-in" all costs incurred by a pipeline for all available services, and charging all shippers equally, regardless of the services actually used by the shippers. In other words, gas sold by a pipeline to an end user at a delivered price as a bundled service contains all costs related to the procurement, transportation, and actual delivery of the gas. Bundled service also assumes that any gas at any location is of equal value and that all costs attached to that gas should be incurred by all customers. Unbundled service calls for the segregation of each service provided by a pipeline, allowing for independent selection and purchase of those services. For example, through unbundling a pipeline's services, a natural gas buyer can elect to purchase gas from a supplier at one location, transport it along the pipeline a short distance (thereby paying a lower transportation rate), and receive the volumes at its designated delivery point. The objective of Orders 436, 500, and 636 was not to change the physical methods of transporting natural gas, but to alter the business activity and the degree of market participation along the interstate pipeline systems. With the constraining regulatory hurdles out of the way, as a result of deregulation, the foundation had been set for one of the most dramatic increases in business activity that any commodity has ever seen.

Chapter 2

The Physical (Cash) Natural Gas Market

The natural gas industry never stops. Natural gas is flowing from wells, moving along pipelines, and burning somewhere at all hours of the day. Therefore, as you would expect, there is never a dull moment in the natural gas market. The type of activity varies throughout the industry, and differs in many ways as well. One certainty does exist—every function in the business is highly dependent on the others in order for the entire industry to function properly. Without producers, there would be no natural gas. Without pipelines, there would be no means of moving natural gas from one location to another. And without end users, there would be no need for natural gas at all! As a general overview, these are the main business activities in the natural gas industry, but on closer examination there are many more functions which keep all of the pieces together. This part of the book covers the business activity and various functions in the physical market, the supply and demand fundamentals of natural gas, the transportation segment, and types of physical transactions between buyers and sellers.

Business Activity

As you will recall from Chapter I, the natural gas industry is comprised of the exploration and production segment and the distribution and sales (consumption) segment. Throughout this chapter, the flow of information presented on the business activity in the physical market will track the flow of natural gas from wellhead to burner—tip!

After a natural gas reservoir is discovered, a production company will drill for and extract the natural gas. From the ground below, the gas emerges into the wellhead. The *wellhead* is the term used for the mechanism which funnels and controls the flow of gas from the ground below up to the surface. It is usually not constructed nor operated by the royalty owner, but rather by a third party, such as a pipeline company or a company specializing solely in the operation of natural gas wells. A royalty owner has the mineral rights to any and all minerals under a designated section of land. There can be, and typically are, several royalty owners for any piece of land. Various types of financing and profit-sharing arrangements exist between royalty owners, operators, and others, but this topic is not within the scope of this text.

From the wellhead, gas enters a small-diameter pipeline system called a *gathering system*. Each wellhead in the vicinity is connected to the gathering system. From there, the natural gas is brought to a central location where it can be processed and then measured by a metering device. Volumes are processed in order to extract liquids and other by-products so the gas will meet standard pipeline specifications. This is usually done by a party other than the operator of the gathering system because there is an active market for bulk quantities of certain by-products, such as butane and propane. The metering device is most important in the context of this text in that this is where title transfer to another party occurs if the gas is resold at this point.

Located on the other side of the processing facility is the *pipeline interconnect*, the point at which the gas is received by a major, larger-diameter pipeline, or *mainline* as they are commonly referred to. This point is called the *receipt point*, of which there are hundreds along a typical pipeline system, connecting gathering systems from various locations. These pipelines can either be interstate or intrastate and typically interconnect with several other major large-diameter pipelines. In fact, the vast pipeline network in North America spans from Mexico to Canada, all four corners of the U.S., and almost everywhere in between. Title transfers can and do occur at thousands of interconnects at varying times, for varying quantities, each headed for potentially different destinations.

The mainline, or pipeline, provides the basic transportation of natural gas from one location to another. Pipelines typically connect regions of supply with market areas, and as such, the direction of flow of natural gas on a mainline system is usually from the supply source to the burner-tip. However, there are some pipelines which have been built to bridge the gap between other pipelines and/or storage facilities.

From an operational standpoint, gas volumes will only flow from an area of high pressure to an area of low pressure. Consequently, to move the gas along a pipeline, *compressor stations* are set up along the way to pressurize the gas so that it will flow to the next compressor station or interconnect. In addition, each pipeline has a maximum capacity of gas it can handle at any one time, and therefore requires that the total volume received at all receipt points should equal the total volume delivered at all interconnects and other delivery points (e.g. burner-tips) along the system.

To help in balancing receipts and deliveries, *storage facilities* are located anywhere from the field (gathering area), along the pipeline systems, to the market areas. Natural gas storage facilities allow a pipeline or other shipper to *inject* or *withdraw* volumes periodically in order to balance any discrepancies between receipts and deliveries. These facilities are usually operated by the pipeline along which they are located, although some third parties also provide storage services. All storage facilities are located underground, of which some are salt-dome caverns and others aquifer caverns. These types of caverns have properties which are excellent for maintaining correct pressures, necessary for operational reasons.

Finally, *end users* are situated at the end of (or various points along) the pipelines. It is at the burner-tip or burning point where the flow of gas stops and is consumed. There are several types of end users, some of which are regulated depending on what type of business they are in. For example, *local distribution companies* (LDCs) provide a pipeline or distribution system with gas supply for consumers in towns and cities. Since LDCs are considered public utilities, they are subject to rate approval and regulation by their state Public Utility Commission (PUC).

Other end users include non-regulated *industrial consumers* which burn natural gas to generate heat to power machines that manufacture their products. Also, *cogeneration* plants utilize natural gas in an energy conversion process whereby water is heated to produce steam that in turn generates electricity. *Commercial* end users burn gas in their place of business to provide spacing heat and heat for hot water, as well as power for air conditioning units. These types of consumers include offices, schools, hotels, and restaurants. *Electric utilities* are the single largest end users of natural gas in terms of the volume of natural gas consumed per user. Electric utilities burn huge quantities of natural gas to generate electricity (much like cogeneration companies), which they sell to all types of electricity buyers, such as residential, industrial, and commercial consumers. But, because they are utilities, the price they can charge for electricity is regulated by their states' PUC. (The electricity market is currently being de-regulated and this may not be the case for long.) Consequently, if natural gas prices rise to the point where it is no longer economical to make the energy conversion based on the price received for the electricity, the utility will switch to alternate fuels such as heavy fuel oil or nuclear energy to generate electricity.

Although they are not technically producers or end users, *marketing companies* play a big role in the business activity along a pipeline. Also known as resellers or third parties, these companies are in the business of capturing profitable opportunities which present themselves in any of the business activities. For example, some marketers provide services, such as acting as agent for a large industrial end user by procuring supply, or as agent for a producer by selling supply. Another opportunity is performing administrative functions for either or both of these parties.

Perhaps the best known function of marketing companies is their role as *trading companies*. Trading companies are those which are in the business of buying and reselling natural gas for a profit. These companies are not paid a fee by anyone but earn the difference or take a loss between what they can buy natural gas for versus what they can sell it for. (Some companies will act as both service marketing companies and trading companies.) As a result of deregulation, any company is free to buy and sell natural gas to anyone. In addition, it is entitled to contract for pipeline capacity on almost any pipeline system. The ability to enter the market with opportunities like these has led to the explosive growth in the number of natural gas trading companies. There are hundreds of these trading companies which provide services such as those

mentioned above, as well as buying and selling with other market participants, trying to "make a spread". A *spread* is the difference between buy price
and sell price. In addition, many producers, LDCs, and electric utilities have
established marketing or trading departments within their respective organizations in order to participate in these profitable opportunities or to special-
ize in administering the services necessary to conduct their business with natural gas.

Each day these trading companies are looking for areas of excess supply or high demand. If they find a region which is temporarily oversupplied, for
example, they can buy and take title of the supply from one counterparty (producer, another trader, or even an end user), and sell and transfer title to another counterparty, capturing a profitable spread in between. Transactions like
this can occur either at the same interconnect, or at another location after
transporting the supply on as few as one or as many as five or more pipelines.
In the end, the goal is to earn a profitable spread.

Service marketing and trading companies are important to the natural
gas industry for several reasons. As a service provider, these companies can
perform many of the necessary administrative business procedures at a low
cost for those companies that don't have established departments, or the
know-how to perform these functions. As traders, they keep the supply and
demand balance in constant equilibrium by searching for profitable arbitrage
opportunities where discrepancies between supply and demand exist. In general, they help the market by providing efficiency, competition, and liquidity.

Beginning with the "Physical Transactions" section of this chapter, and
throughout the remainder of this book, the material presented in this text will
be most useful to those who are more interested in how trading companies,
or those companies which have this function within their organization, conduct their business through the use of trading tools, trading techniques, and
risk management concepts. However, the sections of "Supply Fundamentals",
"Demand Fundamentals", and "Transportation" will introduce the basics that
drive the supply of and demand for natural gas, as well as a discussion on natural gas transportation.

Supply Fundamentals

Natural gas is an underground natural resource. As such, it must be
found, drilled for, and extracted for use, similar to crude oil. In fact, natural gas
is most commonly found wherever oil has been located, as it is a natural
petroleum by-product. Natural gas, however, because of its composition, is
usually found at shallower depths from the ground surface than crude oil, and
is therefore considered easier and less expensive to drill for and extract.
Another characteristic of natural gas which is different from oil is that in its
original state, natural gas is both odorless and colorless. When it has been
brought up to the wellhead and gathering system, a sulfur-like perfume is

added to the pipeline to give it an odor so its presence can be more easily detected by smell in the case of a leak.

Supply Regions

In general, there is an abundance of natural gas supply in North America. The largest U.S. reserves are located underground off the shores of Texas and Louisiana in the Gulf of Mexico. There are also major reserves onshore in both of those states as well as Oklahoma, New Mexico, Colorado, Wyoming, California, and even Pennsylvania and West Virginia to name a few. Perhaps the largest reserve of natural gas in North America, however, is found in the Western Canadian province of Alberta. This supply is also considered to be the least expensive to produce because it is found at extremely shallow depths under ground.

Characteristics of Natural Gas Wells

In terms of production characteristics, natural gas reserves, when discovered, contain varying quantities of natural gas, and have varying "life-spans" depending on how much pressure the reserves are under. In other words, a small reserve that is under high pressure will produce at a faster rate, thereby depleting faster, than would a large reserve under moderate pressure. There really is no way of pumping natural gas out of the ground, it must simply flow from its higher pressure area (underground) to an area of lower pressure (gathering system) until the two pressures are equal. The pressure in the gathering system can, however, be maintained at the lowest possible level, thereby maximizing the amount of natural gas able to be produced from a reserve.

Factors Affecting Supply

The supply of natural gas is essentially dependent on only one factor: price. The higher natural gas prices are, the more incentive producers have to prospect for new reserves. As prices fall, producers will tend to shut-in (close down) wells which are only marginally profitable (i.e. production costs higher relative to other wells) so that maintenance and production costs of these wells do not exceed sales revenues. In addition, the risk of loss increases relative to the potential reward when evaluating new drilling prospects.

Another factor which can sometimes temporarily affect the level of supply is a natural disaster. Due to the vast amount of production which comes from offshore wells in the Gulf of Mexico, hurricanes pose a major threat to the stability of this supply region. Whenever a hurricane threatens the Gulf of Mexico area, producers typically evacuate workers on their offshore production platforms and shut-in supply. The threat itself creates a temporary shortage as it takes time to restart and re-staff these facilities. However, a storm that actually does damage to these rigs, as Hurricane *Andrew* did in 1992, is even more serious. During that storm, several rigs became inoperable and couldn't be restored for almost six months. When news of *Andrew's* damage spread throughout the market, natural gas prices soared as buyers scrambled to replace lost supplies. During the outage, supply from all over the country and even Canada was re-routed through various pipelines to make up for lost supply from the Gulf of Mexico area. Prices around the country continued to rise as demand far outweighed supply. However, by the beginning of 1995 when production from the damaged rigs in the Gulf of Mexico resumed, as well as a 25% surge in natural gas exports from Canada, the supply level caught up with demand and natural gas prices gradually came back to their pre-disaster levels.

On a smaller scale, wellheads tend to "freeze off" during prolonged periods of intense cold weather in some parts of the United States and Canada. When this happens, the wells in a specific production area become inoperable and the supply from that region is temporarily unavailable to the market. As temperatures return to normal, however, production is restored and the gas is once again available to the market. Nonetheless, these factors influence what is a very dynamic, responsive, and unpredictable market.

Demand Fundamentals

The demand side of the market for natural gas is more dynamic than most would think. Natural gas has more uses than just heating and air-conditioning houses or fueling the kitchen stove. Although the primary use for natural gas is as a fuel which is burned to generate heat, there are also other more obscure uses. For example, crude oil producers in California will sometimes use natural gas, because of its capability to be highly pressurized, to extract more crude oil from old, low-pressure wells. This is known as enhanced oil recovery (EOR), and is accomplished by injecting highly pressurized natural gas into the ground underneath the oil reserves in order to increase the crude oil reserve pressure. This use, however, represents a very minuscule portion of overall demand.

Natural Gas Consumption

Industrial companies' consumption represents the largest portion of natural gas demand as they power machines, such as ovens in packaging plants or heavy equipment, to manufacture a product.

Residential consumption of natural gas also accounts for a large portion of total natural gas demand. The use of natural gas by residential users is very straightforward in that it is burned for home heating and is also used as a fuel for stoves, fireplaces, and hot water heating tanks.

Power generation is the third largest market for natural gas. Electric utilities and independent power producers (IPPs), which build and operate cogeneration plants, use natural gas to power gas-fired turbines which generate electricity. The table below shows the breakdown in total consumption by category of usage:

1. Industrial   38%
2. Residential/Commercial   37%
3. Electric Utility Generation   14%
4. Other   11%

Factors Affecting Demand

Unlike the level of supply, which fluctuates mainly as a result of price changes, the level of demand for natural gas rises and falls as a result of changes in price, but for several other reasons as well. By far the most important force which alters the level of demand is Mother Nature. The weather is obviously a major factor, given the large portion of total consumption of natural gas by the residential sector. For instance, winter weather in the Northeast, northern mid-continent, and Pacific Northwestern United States can cause home and office heating demand to easily surpass available supply. Homes and offices which are not heated by natural gas often use electric heating systems, and the utilities and independent power producers that use natural gas to power their generation plants might enter the market to buy gas to meet this demand.

In the summer, demand for natural gas in the Southeast, South Central, and Southwestern United States increases as the pull on electricity demand required to meet home and office air-conditioning demand increases. Because most production of natural gas is in the southern United States, when demand picks up in these regions, supply is held back from the traditional markets, thus creating a tug-of-war effect between these market areas.

In addition to the forces of weather, the general level of activity in the economy can create additional demand or lessen demand for natural gas. If the economy is robust causing demand for steel products, for example, to increase, steel producers will run their factories at maximum capacity to manufacture additional product. Their demand for natural gas increases as they use it to heat ovens to melt more steel during additional work shifts. Similarly, box factories and packaging plants become busier in times of economic expansion and both use natural gas to heat ovens and dryers which are used in the manufacturing of their products. In a broader sense, any businesses which benefit from an expanding economy, and consequently stay open and work longer hours, and rely on natural gas to heat their buildings or power their machines, will consume more gas during these times. Naturally, when the economy is contracting instead of expanding, natural gas demand diminishes, and the chain reaction reverses.

Demand Sensitivity to Price Changes

The demand for natural gas, in terms of consumption, is less sensitive to changes in price than the supply for natural gas is. This is true as prices increase or decrease, but even more apparent when prices decrease. That is, due to the nature of the uses for natural gas, more consumers do not eagerly rush into the market to buy if prices fall. In stark contrast, if prices fall to a certain threshold level, it is not uncommon for producers to shut-in several thousand wells at gathering system interconnects in a matter of a few hours. To illustrate the demand-side sensitivity, let's suppose you live in a cold region of the country and during the winter you keep your house at a comfortable 75 degrees Fahrenheit. If you noticed that natural gas prices had fallen relative to the same time the previous year, would you then use more gas to heat your house at 90 degrees instead? I don't think so. However, if you noticed that prices were higher, you might be more inclined to lower the thermostat in your house to 65 degrees and use your fireplace more often. This reasoning can be applied in the same way to a typical electric utility which burns natural gas to generate electricity. If prices fall, the utility probably won't buy more gas in order to generate excess electricity, unless consumer electricity consumption simultaneously increases, but if prices rise they may chose to switch fuels and burn an alternate fuel that is more economical.

This distinction between the effect of a change in prices on consumption versus demand is important. If prices fall, for example, those who are able to consume more natural gas will most likely do so up to the point at which they have filled that need. Once this need has been filled, it would appear that there should be no more demand. However, because storage facilities can be utilized by end users to smooth out peaks and troughs in their demand profiles, some new buying (demand) will come into the market from those who wish to take advantage of the low prices. Buyers who are anticipating higher consumption requirements in the future are stockpiling supply at current low prices in order to meet that future need. The reverse happens in cases where prices spike higher for short periods of time. If producers view the price spike as only temporary, they can withdrawal supply from a storage facility, in which they had previously injected it during times of lower prices, and sell it.

Transportation

As I mentioned at the beginning of this part of the book, the business activities in the natural gas industry are highly dependent on one another for several reasons—without producers there would be no supply, without end users there would be no demand, and without the pipeline transportation network there would be no means of connecting the supply regions to the market areas. The focus of this section is on natural gas transportation activity in the market, the important services the pipeline companies provide, and how the pipelines perform these services.

Nominations and Nomination Deadlines

A pipeline *nomination* is a notification given by a third party shipper (company transporting on a pipeline) to a pipeline that essentially requests the pipeline recognize, account for, and physically implement a transportation transaction for that shipper. In other words, if a shipper is planning to transport gas supply on a particular pipeline from point A to point B, it must notify that pipeline of its intentions via a nomination. Specifically, a nomination must include the following details to ensure that the pipeline can perform the requested service properly:

1. Shipper's transportation contract number
2. Delivering party's transportation contract number
3. Start date
4. Stop date
5. Shipper's receipt location
6. Shipper's receipt amount
7. Shipper's delivered location
8. Shipper's delivered amount
9. Receiving party's transportation contract number

The *shipper's transportation contract number* designates the account under which the transportation activity will occur. Shippers will often have more than one transportation contract with a pipeline, each of which corresponds to a particular level of service.

The *delivering party's transportation contract number* identifies the source of the supply. This can either be another shipper (title transfer), another pipeline, a gathering system, a processing plant, or a storage facility.

The *start date* and *stop date* notify the pipeline of the duration of the transportation service. It is understood by both the shipper and the pipeline that the exact hour the gas supply will begin flowing on the start date and the exact hour the gas supply will cease flowing on the stop date corresponds to the pipelines predetermined measuring period defined in its tariff.

The *shipper's receipt location* designates a meter number (interconnect with another pipeline, compressor station, etc.) where the pipeline will be receiving the gas for the shipper's account from the delivering party.

The *shipper's receipt amount* is the amount of gas the shipper is requesting from its supply source each day for the duration of the service. The amount is expressed as MMBtu per day, and is assumed to flow at a constant rate for the entire day.

The *shipper's delivered location* designates the meter number where the pipeline will be delivering the shipper's gas supply.

The *shipper's delivered amount* is the amount of gas the shipper is expecting the pipeline to deliver at the delivery point. In most cases, the delivered amount will be less than the receipt amount because pipelines charge shipper's "in kind" for fuel required to run the gas-fired compressor stations along the pipeline's system. For example, if the receipt amount at point A is 10,000 MMBtu/d, and the fuel required to transport to point B is 5%, the delivered amount will only be 9,500 MMBtu/d. Fuel percentages vary depending on the distance between receipt and delivery points.

The *receiving party's transportation contract number* identifies the destination for the gas supply. This can either be another shipper (title transfer), another pipeline, a gathering system, a processing plant, or a storage facility.

Because natural gas transactions are done on a daily basis, natural gas pipelines monitor their systems on a day-to-day basis as well. Although some pipelines choose slightly different hours, the times that physical operators of wellheads, gathering systems, and the pipelines themselves measure and account for volumes flowing through their respective systems typically begins at 7 a.m. central time and ends at 7 a.m. the following day. As I mentioned earlier, natural gas is in continuous flow unless a well is "shut-in." As such, in order to know what volume to expect to flow through their systems and whose account it is for, pipeline operators require nominations by a certain time on the day before the gas is to begin flowing. The typical nomination deadline is 10 a.m. central time for gas to flow the following day. As a result of these nomination deadlines, trading activity is busiest in the early morning hours as traders conduct their business for the following day. However, trading activity, albeit at a slower pace, continues throughout the day for subsequent day's transactions, or transactions made for longer durations.

Confirming, Scheduling, Allocating, and Balancing

Confirming. Once the pipeline has received a nomination from a shipper, the pipeline goes through a confirmation procedure. A pipeline confirms a shipper's nomination by "matching" *all* of the details in the confirmation with the same specifics in the nominations from the delivering party (or parties) and receipt party (or parties). That is, in order for a shipper's nomination to be confirmed, the delivering party's details must match the shipper's receiving details, and the receiving party's details must match the shipper's delivery details. For example, let's suppose a shipper submits the following nomination to a pipeline:

1.	Shipper's transportation contract number	1234
2.	Delivering party's transportation contract number	1111
3.	Start date	02/10/96
4.	Stop date	02/15/96
5.	Shipper's receipt location	# A001
6.	Shipper's receipt amount	10,000/d
7.	Shipper's delivered location	# B002
8.	Shipper's delivered amount	9,500/d
9.	Receiving party's transportation contract number	2222

The delivering party's nomination would have to match the corresponding details. It should look like the nomination below:

1.	Shipper's transportation contract number	1111
2.	Delivering party's transportation contract number	N/A
3.	Start date	02/10/96
4.	Stop date	N/A
5.	Shipper's receipt location	N/A
6.	Shipper's receipt amount	N/A
7.	Shipper's delivered location	# A001
8.	Shipper's delivered amount	10,000/d
9.	Receiving party's transportation contract number	1234

(*Note: "N/A" has been inserted because these items are not relevant to matching up the source (delivering party) with the shipper. The pipeline is only concerned with the items which correspond to those on the shipper's nomination. The start date is the only date the pipeline is concerned with because the nomination will "roll over" day-to-day until either the delivering party terminates it, which requires another nomination, or the stop date on the shipper's nomination is reached, whichever comes first.*)

As you can see, the shipper's corresponding details match with the delivering party's. From this information, the pipeline can confirm *half* of the nomination (The shipper is correctly requesting 10,000 MMBtu/d from contract number 1111 at meter A001 starting on 02/10/96 and stopping on 02/15/96.) To confirm the shipper's delivery side of the nomination, the nomination received by the pipeline from the receipt party (destination) must match the corresponding details on the shipper's nomination. It should look like the nomination below:

1.	Shipper's transportation contract number	2222
2.	Delivering party's transportation contract number	1234
3.	Start date	02/10/96
4.	Stop date	N/A
5.	Shipper's receipt location	# B002
6.	Shipper's receipt amount	9,500/d
7.	Shipper's delivered location	N/A
8.	Shipper's delivered amount	N/A
9.	Receiving party's transportation contract number	N/A

As you can see, the shipper's corresponding details match with the receiving party's (destination). From this information, the pipeline can confirm the nomination (i.e. the shipper is correctly receiving 10,000 MMBtu/d from contract number 1111 at meter A001 starting on 02/10/96, and the shipper is correctly delivering 9,500 MMBtu/d to contract number 2222 at meter B002 starting on 02/10/96. Again, the start date is the only date the pipeline is concerned with because the nomination will "roll over" day-to-day until either the delivering party or the receiving party terminates it, which requires additional nominations, or the stop date on the shipper's nomination is reached, whichever comes first.

If any of the relevant information from either the shipper's delivering party or the shipper's receiving party does not match the information on the shipper's nomination, the nomination will not be confirmed. At that point, the pipeline will contact the shipper (or the shipper will be notified electronically if the pipeline utilizes an electronic nominations system) and ask the shipper to re-submit the nomination with the correct information, or contact the party where the discrepancy exists and ask that party (or parties if both are nominating incorrectly) to re-submit the nomination(s) to the pipeline.

Scheduling. When a confirmation has been issued for a nomination, the pipeline then *schedules* the gas to flow. This is the process whereby the pipeline notifies its operations personnel that the pipeline should expect the amount of gas in the shipper's nomination to flow through the shipper's designated receipt meter and the shipper's designated delivery meter on the start date, and every day thereafter until further notice is given. There is typically more gas flowing through meters other than the amount in one shipper's nomination, so the pipeline operators will designate the amount specified in the shipper's nomination at a particular meter as gas supply intended for the shipper's account, once the nominations group has scheduled it. After the shipper's receipt and delivery has been scheduled, most pipelines will furnish a report to all the parties in the transaction that the scheduling process has been completed successfully. The transaction, however is not yet complete.

Allocating. Scheduling is only what the pipeline *expects* to happen on its system. Because the measuring period covers a full 24-hour time frame, pipeline operators do not know what gas supply was *actually* received and delivered until the day after it is scheduled to flow. For this reason, the pipeline must *allocate* the amount of gas that actually flowed through a meter (or meters) among the various shippers which nominated gas at that point for that day. Allocations are typically done by first granting full amount scheduled by those shippers utilizing firm transportation contracts, and then prorating the remaining amount among shippers utilizing interruptible contracts. For example, let's suppose the total amount of gas which actually flowed through a particular meter on a given day was 90,000 MMBtu but the pipeline had scheduled 100,000 MMBtu to flow. If two firm shippers had each requested 25,000 MMBtu, the pipeline would allocate that amount to each firm shipper. The remaining 40,000 MMBtu would be prorated. Following is a sample of how the pipeline would allocate this particular meter for that day, assuming the following initially scheduled amounts by shipper:

Shipper	Scheduled	Allocated	
Firm shipper 1	25,000	25,000	
Firm shipper 2	25,000	25,000	
Interruptible shipper 1	30,000	24,000	(30,000÷50,000*40,000)
Interruptible shipper 2	15,000	12,000	(15,000÷50,000*40,000)
Interruptible shipper 3	5,000	4,000	(5,000÷50,000, *40,000)
Total	100,000	90,000	

Allocating is done at all meters on a pipeline's system. As such, pipelines are continuously measuring and accounting for the amount of gas scheduled to flow and for what actually flows through their respective pipelines. That is, the pipeline is constantly juggling scheduled amounts versus allocated amounts, always lagging behind by one full day.

Balancing. In addition to juggling between scheduled and received volumes, pipelines must also balance scheduled and allocated receipts into its system with scheduled and allocated deliveries out of its system. As a result, a shipper's transportation activity is subject to the integrity of a pipeline's operations system, as well as the accuracy of its measuring systems. If a pipeline has allocated a lower received amount to a shipper than was scheduled, the pipeline will typically "cut" the delivery (or deliveries) made by the shipper by the same amount. For example, in terms of scheduling, if a shipper nominates a 10,000 MMBtu receipt, but nominates a 12,000 MMBtu delivery, the pipeline will only schedule a delivery of 9,500 MMBtu (assuming 5% fuel "in kind") in order to avoid "throwing" the pipeline out of balance. However, in terms of allocating, if the shipper nominates a 10,000 MMBtu receipt, and nominates a 9,500 delivery (assuming 5% fuel "in kind"), but the pipeline actually only receives 9,900 MMBtu (allocated) at the shipper's receipt point and actually delivers 9,700 MMBtu (allocated) at the shipper's delivery point, the shipper will have a 300 MMBtu imbalance with the pipeline for that day.

Most pipelines allow for a 3% scheduled imbalance tolerance for any given day if the pipeline can physically handle the impact, or if the shipper has an existing imbalance that it wishes to work off by overreceiving or over-delivering for one or more days until the imbalance is eliminated. However, if imbalances are not eliminated by the end of the month, the pipeline will penalize the shipper for the imbalance. Shippers are penalized for imbalances by what is known as a "cash out" price established by the pipelines. For example, if a shipper has under-delivered (resulting in a long imbalance position), the pipeline will "cash out" the imbalance by paying the shipper a discount to market prices for the amount of the imbalance for that month. Similarly, if a

shipper has over-delivered (resulting in a short imbalance position), the pipeline will "cash out" the imbalance by requiring the shipper to pay a premium to market prices for the amount of the imbalance for that month. This "cash out" concept provides an incentive for shippers to keep receipts and deliveries in balance.

Transportation Contracts

There are two basic types of transportation contracts under which shippers can arrange for transportation service. Aside from variations in terms of length of service, transportation contracts can be either firm or interruptible. *Firm transportation* is that form of service which has priority over interruptible and, in addition, cannot be disrupted by the pipeline while it is in use for any reason, other than natural disasters. *Interruptible* transportation service, on the other hand, has low priority in terms of reliability because it can be disrupted by the pipeline while it is in use for any reason, including natural disasters. Before covering the rate structures of firm and interruptible transportation contracts, I would like to explain some of the reasons why pipelines often disrupt a shipper's transportation service, other than natural disasters.

Each pipeline, specifically each segment of a pipeline, is capable of containing a maximum amount of gas at any one time. This is known as the pipeline or pipeline segment's maximum *capacity*. The maximum capacity of a pipeline segment depends on several factors, the most important of which is the pressure in that segment. When a pipeline segment is at maximum capacity, the pressure in that segment is highest. Alternatively, when a pipeline segment has excess capacity, the pressure in that segment is lower than when it is at maximum capacity. Because natural gas moves along a pipeline system by flowing from an area of high pressure to one of lower pressure, a pipeline that is at maximum capacity cannot receive additional gas, but can deliver it at an increased rate. Similarly, a pipeline which has excess capacity can receive additional gas, but can only deliver it at a normal or below normal rate. Therefore, if many shippers are utilizing a segment of pipe, and each is attempting to receive more gas than delivered, the pressure in that segment of the pipeline will increase, pushing that segment to maximum capacity. In addition, a pipeline segment's pressure can also increase if deliveries fall short of receipts. A pipeline segment's pressure tends to increase when demand is extremely low (deliveries less than receipts), or extremely high (all firm shippers are utilizing available capacity). When this happens, the pipeline is forced to cut interruptible shipper's received and delivered volumes until the pressure in that segment normalizes.

The rate structures of firm and interruptible transportation contracts are similar in some ways, but very different in others. Under both firm and interruptible transportation contracts, shippers must pay what is known as a *commodity rate*.(All pipeline rates are expressed in $/MMBtu.) This is a flexible rate in that it is only charged when gas is transported, and can vary depending on the time of the year and the distance the gas is being transported. In addition, firm and interruptible shippers must pay certain surcharges which can vary depending on the specific pipeline. These include a Gas Research Institute charge (GRI), an actual cost adjustment charge (ACA), *take-or-pay* charges, and others. The GRI fee varies between $0.0085/MMBtu and $0.0088/MMBtu, the ACA fee varies between $0.0022/MMBtu and $0.0023/MMBtu, and the others are very pipeline specific. However, some pipelines have waived the ACA and GRI fees from their rate schedules. In addition to the commodity charge and surcharges, both firm and interruptible shippers may pay "in kind" for fuel charges. (Delivered volume will be less than received volume by a fuel percentage.)

The rate mechanism which differentiates a firm transportation contract from an interruptible contract is called a reservation charge. This represents a "fixed" charge in that it is assessed on the total purchased capacity, whether or not gas actually flows under the contract. This reservation charge is what gives firm transportation priority over interruptible when "cuts" have to be made by a pipeline due to capacity constraints, and can vary depending on the distance between receipt and delivery points, time of the year, and the amount of capacity purchased. Capacity for longer distances and for larger volumes is typically less per unit than shorter hauls of smaller volume. Therefore, in addition to a commodity charge, applicable surcharges, and an "in kind" fuel charge, the firm shipper pays a reservation charge which guarantees reliable transportation service (except in the event of a natural disaster). However, if the transportation capacity is not fully utilized, the firm shipper is still obligated to pay the reservation charge, whereas the interruptible shipper can elect not to use the service and therefore not incur any costs.

Transportation Rates

As briefly explained in the previous section, commodity charges and reservation charges set by the pipelines can vary depending on the time of the year, the distance the gas is being transported, and the volume of capacity contracted for (firm service only). But how do the pipelines structure their rates in such a way that covers the pipeline's cost of doing business as well as earn a favorable return? Although this subject is worthy of an entire chapter, I will attempt to summarize the basic concepts behind how the interstate pipelines establish their transportation rates. Because the intrastate pipelines are not regulated by the FERC, their rate structures and how they establish them are somewhat ambiguous, although similar interstate concepts are often used.

First and foremost, the pipeline is most concerned with maintaining a fully utilized system. That is, similar to the airline industry, the goal of a pipeline company is to keep the pipeline as full as possible without damaging the integrity of the system. From an investment perspective, when a pipeline is at maximum capacity, the pipeline should, as a result, be earning as much money as it possibly can. From an operational perspective, if the pipeline has excess capacity, resulting in lower pipeline pressures, it may not be able to adequately meet its obligated deliveries.

However, operational flexibility must be considered when strategizing over how to design a rate structure. In other words, the pipeline cannot sell only firm transportation, because if pressures are not accurately maintained at an optimum level, the pipeline would have to disrupt some of the firm transportation contracts in order to balance its system from day to day. For this reason, some capacity must not be sold firm, but interruptible so that the pipeline can swing on these contracts to maintain its flexibility.

Although there is no precise formula by which pipelines determine how much capacity should be sold firm and how much should be sold interruptible, a pipeline would generally prefer to sell more than 50% of its maximum capacity under long-term (five years or longer) firm contracts, and the remaining capacity under interruptible contracts. Ideally, the pipeline can cover its cost of doing business through these long-term firm contracts, and rely on the revenue from interruptible contracts to make its profit.

Although the rates that interstates can charge for transportation service must be approved through a rate filing with the FERC, the rates that the shippers are willing to pay ultimately determines what the pipelines can charge. Transportation sales representatives typically design firm transportation rate structures for those supply and market paths where they know the pipeline's capacity is in high demand. Additionally, the pipeline representatives avoid selling firm capacity in these areas for segregated times of the year, but instead encourage firm shippers to purchase firm capacity for the entire year or years so that the pipeline is assured of maintaining transportation volumes through those months when demand is low (e.g., summertime in the northeastern United States), and the shipper is assured of the reliability in service during those months when demand is high. In general, pipelines typically push to sell long-term firm capacity when demand for natural gas is expected to be high, and hold off in times when demand is expected to be low.

Once the desired amount of firm transportation capacity has been contracted out (or if it hasn't been sold at a justifiable price), the pipelines face the task of filling the remaining capacity through interruptible contracts. Because there is no monetary obligation for shippers that contract for interruptible capacity (other than standard credit evaluation), shippers typically hold interruptible transportation contracts on several, if not all, major pipelines. To entice these shippers to utilize their interruptible agreements, thereby generating revenue, pipelines will often discount their maximum published commodity tariff rates, depending on the status of the supply and demand balance on their respective systems. For example, if a particular segment of a pipeline has lost pressure due to a change in supply or demand, the pipeline transportation representatives will contact active interruptible shippers via telephone or an electronic bulletin board service (EBB) and offer discounted commodity transportation rates for that segment to entice these shippers to transport gas across the system. In general, wherever and whenever excess capacity exists that is not required for operational purposes, pipelines will negotiate the commodity transportation rates on a case-by-case basis to entice shippers to utilize the capacity.

By combining a mix of firm transportation contracts, interruptible contracts, and even storage facilities for operational purposes, pipelines can provide various levels of transportation services, maintain system integrity (flexibility and reliability), and earn a respectful profit.

Capacity Release and Trading

Due to changing market dynamics and requests from shippers, interstate pipelines were permitted to allow for capacity release among their firm transportation shippers in April of 1992. *Capacity release* refers only to firm transportation capacity and is the option whereby a firm shipper can assign its firm transportation capacity on a pipeline to a third party that is willing to pay all or some portion of the reservation charge as well as any commodity charges, applicable surcharges, and fuel "in kind" charges. As the term plainly describes, this effectively "releases" the original firm shipper from its obligation to pay the pipeline for firm transportation service, by assigning (or selling) that capacity to another party. Although deals can be negotiated exclusively between shippers, the preferred method of releasing capacity is through a closed bidding process on the pipeline's EBB (electronic bulletin board) wherein the buyer submits a percentage of maximum firm transportation rate bid to the seller of the firm capacity. The buyer with the highest percentage bid will be assigned that firm capacity.

Capacity release not only enables the original firm shipper to recover some, if not all, of the fixed reservation charge for its excess firm capacity, but it also enables other shippers to buy firm transportation for only those times when they feel that firm capacity would be a necessity. In other words, if a shipper knew that it needed to transport a minimum of 10,000 MMBtu/d for the month of October, and the shipper wanted to be absolutely certain that this amount would be transported to its market area customer for the entire month without disruption, the shipper could monitor the pipeline's EBB and buy 10,000 MMBtu/d of released capacity for that month only, instead of signing a one or three year long-term firm transportation contract with the pipeline. As such, capacity release has allowed for a more efficient means of maximizing the use of a pipeline's various levels of service.

In summary, the natural gas pipeline transportation network is essentially the backbone of the natural gas industry. Through various levels of service, and flexibility in providing these services, the pipeline network efficiently and cost effectively links regions of supply with market areas. Without natural gas pipelines, the natural gas market simply wouldn't exist.

Physical Transaction Types
Natural Gas Physical Trading Contracts

Natural gas is bought and sold under different types of contracts, or agreements. Each contract, however, references the following at least standard specifications:

1. buyer
2. seller
3. price
4. amount (expressed as amount per day)
5. receipt / delivery point location (title transfer point)
6. tenure (expressed as number of days beginning on a specified date)
7. terms and conditions

The list above is somewhat self-explanatory with the exception of the last item—special terms and conditions. The special terms and conditions section of most contracts typically outlines details such as payment dates, quality specifications, and specifics regarding performance, just to name a few. There are three types of performance obligations that differentiate contracts. Their importance determines which contract is appropriate for a given transaction: interruptible ("swing"), baseload, or firm.

Swing Contracts

Under an interruptible contract, the buyer and seller agree on a specific price and amount in the transaction, but limit the term of the transaction to as short as one day or as long as the entire month or days remaining in a month. (Most interruptible contracts are used on a day-to-day time frame.) In addition, both parties agree that neither party is obligated to deliver or receive the exact volume agreed to. That is, if the full amount of gas is not delivered by the seller, or taken by the buyer, that party is neither financially nor physically responsible for making up the difference. Also, both parties agree that at the end of the initial term of the agreement, neither party is obligated to renew the agreement for the same price, volume, delivery point, or tenure. As a result of their flexibility, interruptible transactions are usually referred to in the industry as "swing" deals. (i.e., In a day-to-day interruptible contract, both price and volume can swing up and down. This type of arrangement is used in instances where supply or demand is unreliable.)

Baseload Contracts

Baseload agreements are similar to interruptible agreements in that each party agrees that neither party is obligated to deliver or receive the volume in the transaction. However, although neither party is legally obligated to the volume, it is a general understanding among natural gas market participants that each party in a baseload transaction will, on a best-effort basis only, deliver and take the volume in the transaction. (There is no legal definition of "best-effort." As such, performance under baseload contracts is a matter of the personal and professional relationship between the buyer and seller.) In the matter of price, it is also a general understanding between buyer and seller that neither party will terminate the agreement due to changing market prices after the transaction has been done. This is also not a legal obligation. (Although baseload deals can be as short in tenure as one day, the common practice is to transact for an entire month or the remaining days in a month.) Like interruptible transactions, neither party is obligated to renew the agreement after the initial term has expired.

Firm Contracts

In stark contrast to both interruptible and baseload contracts, firm contracts have legal recourse embedded within them for instances where either party fails to take or deliver the agreed upon volume at the agreed upon price for the agreed upon tenure in the contract. This type of contract has adapted its name from a similar contract used in the earlier stages of the natural gas market as a take-or-pay contract, with one change. Earlier take-or-pay contracts required the buyer to either take the total volume under the transaction and pay for it accordingly, or pay the total cost for the amount of gas transacted for even if the total volume was not actually taken. Firm transactions, however, have been slightly modified in that in the event either the buyer fails to take the total amount of supply on a day-by-day basis or the seller fails to make the total supply available on a day-by-day basis, the defaulting party is only required to pay the difference between the replacement sale price (when buyer defaults), or the replacement purchase price (when seller defaults), and the contract price in the original transaction. Because of this financial ramification in failure to perform, these contracts are only used in transactions where the supply and demand for the gas is expected to be 100% reliable.

Chapter 3

The Financial Natural Gas Market

Value

Like any other freely traded commodity, natural gas has a monetary and a utilitarian value. Whether burned by a residential user to provide heat or produced by an E & P company to sell for money, natural gas is a valuable commodity. After all, it would be of no use to anyone if it didn't have some kind of value. The utilitarian value of natural gas is that it is a fuel which can be burned to provide heat for various uses.

In the United States, natural gas derives its value from its British thermal unit (Btu) content, or heating capability. (Canada uses gigajoules as a measurement of heating content.) *Webster's Dictionary* defines a *British thermal unit* as, "a unit of heat equal to about 252 calories; quantity of heat required to raise the temperature of one pound of water one degree Fahrenheit." Although it can vary slightly depending on what region of the country the gas is produced in, the Btu content of all natural gas is considered to be equal after it has been processed and enters a main pipeline system. Volumetrically, natural gas is measured in cubic feet (cf) on a 24-hour flowing basis, and consequently a standard conversion was adopted whereby 1 cf = 1,000 Btus, which allows for natural gas to be bought and sold in terms of its Btu value.

Perceived vs. Market Value

The monetary value of natural gas is reflected in terms of its price. The price of natural gas, like any other freely traded commodity or security, fluctuates when the perceived value of that product changes. The difference in opinion between buyers and sellers over what the perceived value of a commodity or security should be is what constitutes a market. The perceived value of a commodity or security is what someone thinks it should be worth. The price, or market value, is a reflection of what the majority of the market perceives to be the value of the product, and is what the commodity is actually worth at that specific point in time.

The supply and demand balance of any commodity or security is constantly moving into or out of equilibrium as a result of changes in the opinion of the majority of market participants regarding the commodity's perceived value. For example, if the perceived value of natural gas is greater than the current price, buyers who share this opinion will buy at current prices and continue buying at higher prices until its market value climbs to what they perceive its value to be. Similarly, if the market value of natural gas is greater than what the majority of market participants perceive its value to be, sellers who share this opinion will sell at current prices and continue selling at lower prices until its market value falls to their perceived value.

This is where the presence of trading companies can be most appreciated. By continuously searching for discrepancies between supply and demand, or discrepancies between market participant's perceived values of natural gas, traders are invariably pushing the market into equilibrium. As a result, trading companies lend some structure or organization to this concept and help maintain an orderly market.

Pricing and Trading

Pricing Format

The standard pricing format for natural gas is in dollars and cents per MMBtu to flow on a daily basis. For example, the following is a typical transaction on an agreed upon deal between a buyer and a seller: "I will agree to pay you $2.10 for 10,000 MMBtus per day for Monday through Friday." The buyer is agreeing to buy 10,000 mmBtus per day, at a price of $2.10 per MMBtu, for each day Monday through Friday. The total size of the trade is 50,000 MMBtus for a total cost to the buyer of $105,000. The shorthand lingo for this trade might sound like this: "I will agree to pay you $2.10 for 10 million a day, Monday through Friday." Even though the buyer and seller are trading 10,000 MMBtus per day, and exchanging a price based on MMBtus, they still speak in terms of volume when trading. That is, 10,000 MMBtu/d is the volumetric equivalent of 10 MMcf/d, or "10 million cubic feet per day." The only logical explanation for this is that natural gas was originally traded in volumes and not Btus, and that tradition has carried on only in this spoken lingo. The trade would still be booked and accounted for as 10,000 MMBtu/d. It is still not common practice to speak in terms of Btus when trading, only in recording and accounting for transactions.

The Daily Market for Natural Gas

In the day-to-day market for physical natural gas, buyers and sellers still conduct the majority of their transactions with each other over the telephone. Electronic Bulletin Boards (EBBs) have recently been established whereby physical trades can be cleared at a few major trading points by third party operators. Natural gas traders have lists of contacts at other companies whom they know are traders of gas on a particular pipeline, at a specific point, or in a designated region of the country. It is through these contacts that most transactions are done and market information is disseminated.

For example, if a trader receives a phone call from an LDC buyer who is looking for 10,000 MMBtu/d at Transco Station 65 (Zone 3) for the following day and is willing to pay $2.30, he will immediately begin calling other traders and producers who regularly buy and sell on that pipeline at that location. If the trader thinks he can make a $0.05 / MMBtu margin, he tells the other traders he is, "$2.25 bid for 10,000 MMBtu/d on Transco at Station 65." Assuming he is successful in paying $2.25 for the gas, he calls the LDC back and agrees to sell to them at $2.30, thereby making $500 on the trade. It can be (and sometimes is) that simple.

Bid-Week Trading Ritual

Although the daily market for natural gas is active, the majority of gas trading occurs during the last week of each month. This period of time is known in the industry as *bid-week*. It is the time when market participants buy and sell the majority of their gas requirements and available volumes of gas for the following month. Even though gas transactions are done in terms of volume per day, the standard industry practice is to deal for a month at a time. During bidweek, trading volume is heaviest as producers are trying to sell their core supply, end users are trying to buy for their core needs, and marketing companies are trying to get in between the two. *Core* refers to that supply or demand which is 100% reliable each day for the entire month. The most common pricing method traded during this time period is fixed-price. However, there are other forms of pricing which are gaining popularity and are becoming more widely used.

Price Discovery in the Cash Market

Although there are many different pricing structures, buying and selling natural gas at fixed prices is most common structure. Prior to April, 1990, and to some degree today, buyers and sellers would use the telephone to call other traders in order to obtain pricing information. If a trader had supply to sell, the trader would have to make several phone calls to would-be buyers in order to discover the market price at that time. Once the trader felt comfortable that enough buyers had been surveyed and he or she had a good feel for the market, the trader would then sell the gas to the highest paying buyer. This method of price discovery worked well, and is still used today to some degree, but only for trades of short duration.

The daily or *spot market* for natural gas is the most active and therefore the most liquid in which to trade. As such, price discovery for spot market transactions is relatively simple (a few phone calls) and yields prices which are tightly clustered around a certain price. For example, after making phone calls to 10 different traders you know who are buyers and sellers for the next day, you might find the following: three buyers at $1.99, two buyers at $1.98, three sellers at $2.01, and two sellers at $2.02. As you can see, they are all relatively close to one another, and they are all tightly clustered around $2.00.

Price discovery for trades of longer duration or even deferred start dates is not nearly as simple. Let's suppose one needed to buy natural gas beginning two months from today for a period of six months thereafter. Using the traditional telephone survey method, you talk with 10 different traders who are buyers and sellers for that time period and discover the following: one buyer at $2.11, one buyer at $2.00, one buyer at $2.17, one buyer at $1.97, two sellers with small volume at $2.33, and four sellers that couldn't come up with a price at the time. As you can see, all but two traders had different perceptions of what the value of natural gas should be for that specific time period. Although this method used to work, it was costly and inefficient. The market lacked an efficient and simple way to value natural gas for any period of time in the future. The natural gas industry needed tools for help with price discovery and price risk management.

Chapter 4

Hedging and Trading Instruments

Before exploring the different financial instruments and trading concepts in natural gas, it is necessary to address some of the terminology and trading lingo to more easily understand these topics. The first section will explore the more common important terms and phrases used when trading commodities and securities, in general, and those terms more specifically used in the natural gas market. The remaining sections will cover the popular trading tools used in trading natural gas.

Financial Market Terminology
Derivatives

In financial markets, a *derivative* is a trading instrument, the value of which is determined from the value or values of one or more physical commodities and or financial securities underlying the derivative. The physical commodity and/or financial security from which a derivative obtains its value is called the *underlying* commodity or security. As financial instruments, derivatives can be traded in much the same way as the underlying commodity or security, but most are traded in the over-the-counter (OTC) market. (The OTC market refers to a collection of traders, brokers, and other market participants which are interested in a given commodity, security, or derivative, and trade it among themselves and not on an exchange.) Unlike their respective underlying commodities or securities, however, derivatives are sometimes preferred as a trading tool for their leveraging capability.

Leverage, in financial terms, is the effect of magnifying the outcome of an investment through the use of borrowed funds (credit), or a small (relative to the total cost of the investment) down payment. A home mortgage, for instance, is used for leveraging the anticipated future earnings of a home buyer so he or she can purchase a house which costs more money than he or she currently has available. The return on a leveraged investment can be either positive or negative for an investor, but is sure to be a much larger gain or loss than had the investment not been leveraged.

Due to the ill fortunes of some investors who were not aware of the power of leverage, derivatives have recently been categorized as dangerous, high-risk investments. In fact, if the risk of leverage and other factors typical of many derivatives are not fully understood, a derivative trade can surprise even the most veteran of traders. For example, if a investor contemplates buying a derivative that will return a 25% profit if one out of four different events occurs, but can result in a 100% loss of capital if none of the four events occurs, the investor may view this as a good risk reward scenario for an investment. However, once the trade is executed, and the investor learns that an active market for this particular derivative doesn't exist and that in order to get out of the position, he would have to either pay an amount of money which would result in a 400% loss of his capital, or keep the trade on until it either returns the 25% on his capital, or loses 100% of it. As you can see, although the investor felt the initial risk reward potential was worthy of his investment, he was not aware that once the trade was put on, he would be stuck with it, regardless of whether or not he wanted it after all.

On the other hand, derivatives can be helpful and powerful trading tools if used properly and fully understood. For example, a mortgage company can offer a home buyer either a fixed-percentage-rate mortgage, or an adjustable-rate mortgage (i.e. one in which the percentage rate of which fluctuates monthly according to the interest rate market). Through the use of a derivative known as a swap, the mortgage company could then convert the financing choice of the home buyer into one which matches its own portfolio. In other words, if the home buyer elects an adjustable rate mortgage, but the mortgage company is paying a fixed rate for the money it is borrowing from a bank to lend to the home buyer, a swap can be used to convert the variable rate payment received from the buyer into a fixed-rate payment so the mortgage company is not exposed to falling market interest rates. The most common use for derivatives is for uses such as this, more commonly known as *hedging risk*.

Hedging

In general, the term *hedging* is used when describing the purpose of entering a transaction with the intent of offsetting risk from another related transaction. For example, buying insurance is a hedge against the risk of paying the entire cost of replacing or repairing something that is stolen or damaged. For instance, a fire insurance policy will pay for repairing or replacing a house that is burned in a fire. Also, the mortgage company in the previous section can hedge it's risk between an adjustable interest rate and a fixed interest rate by hedging that risk with a certain type of swap.

In the commodities and securities markets, a hedge is a transaction entered into for the purpose of protecting the value of a commodity or security from adverse price movement by entering an offsetting position in a related commodity or security. Natural gas producers, for example, will often hedge against falling natural gas prices by selling natural gas futures contracts, hoping to profit by buying them back at a lower price, in order to offset the lower prices it will receive in the cash market. Similarly, natural gas end users hedge against rising prices by buying futures contracts, hoping to profit by selling them back at a higher price, in order to offset the higher prices it will pay in the cash market.

Lingo in the Financial Markets

H*edging* and *derivative* are just two of the many terms which are part of the trading lingo that is spoken in the commodity and securities markets. These convenient shorthand terms and phrases evolved from the need for a speedy and concise means by which traders could convey ideas pertaining to a particular trade or market. This industry jargon enables market participants to communicate accurately, effectively, and without hesitation.

It is fairly safe to say that in almost every market, brokers and traders will quote a given commodity or security by first quoting the highest price at which buyers are currently willing to pay (the bid), followed by the lowest price at which sellers are currently willing to sell (the offer). This is called a *bid/offer spread*, or *market*, for that commodity or security.

If a trader is not making a market, but instead wants to obtain one, either OTC or on an exchange, even though the last price traded on an exchange is printed on a quote screen, good commodity and securities traders will always ask for the *market* for that particular product that they are interested in before placing a buy or sell order. They do this for four main reasons; First, on an exchange traded commodity or security, the last price posted on the screen does not necessarily reflect the true current market; second, most quote screens do not show the current bid/offer spread; third, in the case of some OTC derivatives like natural gas swaps, there are no quote screens to rely on for pricing, but rather OTC brokers who are in constant contact with swap traders keeping up with the most current bid/offer spread; and fourth to possibly obtain additional market information other than price, such as how many buyers there are vs. sellers, or how much volume is on the bid versus on the offer.

Unless specified otherwise, the price quoted by futures brokers and the style in which it is quoted is usually in a shorthand version, leaving it up to the trader to know the full *handle* (root price), and also that the term *bid* means "buy price" and *at* is short for "offered at-." For instance, if a trader wanted to know the current market for Feb. natural gas futures, he or she would call a broker and ask, "How is the market for Feb. natgas?" A good broker would reply, "Feb. natgas is two bid at three. There are 200 on the bid and 50 on the offer." An even shorter version would be, "two bid at three—200 by 50." The shorthand, "two bid at three" could mean $2.02 bid, offered at $2.03, or $2.32 bid, offered at $2.33, or any other handles that end in two and three. As long as the trader is familiar with where the market is, the use of shorthand quoting is fine. If however, a trader is not familiar with the market, or the market price has changed dramatically, the trader should ask the broker for the "full handle".

Placing an Order or Transacting a Trade

When giving an order to a broker or when transacting with another trading counterparty, the following generic speaking format is recommended and most commonly used:

"PAY (price) FOR (volume)," or "SELL (volume) AT (price)."

For example, if you want to buy 25 Feb. natural gas futures contracts, the conversation with your broker should sound something like this:

You:	"Hi. My account number is 1234. How is Feb. natgas, please?"
Broker:	"Feb natgas is two bid at three—100 by 50."
You:	"Please pay three for 25."
Broker:	"OK. I'm paying $2.03 for 25 Feb. natgas?"
You:	"Yes. That's correct."
	(Broker executes order.)
Broker:	"OK. Your order is filled. You paid $2.03 for 25 Feb. natgas."
You:	"Thank you."
Broker:	"Thank you."

Although there are other types of orders which can be placed with exchange brokers such as *limit, stop-loss, good-until-canceled,* and so on, they are not covered within the scope of this text. Please refer to any number of futures trading handbooks or reference guides which detail these and many other types of orders that exchange brokers can execute.

Other Shorthand Phrases

As a final note on trading lingo, quick phrases are used to describe the general notion of buying and selling. If, after obtaining the current market for a given commodity or security, a trader pays the offer price, the trader has *lifted the offer* in the market. If the trader sells at the bid price, the trader is said to have *hit the bid* in the market. These phrases might come from the fact that the offer is a higher price than the middle of the bid/offer spread and the bid is a lower price than the middle of the market. Therefore, a trader must sometimes lift the offer from its resting place to buy from a seller, and similarly, a trader must sometimes come down and hit the bid to give it to the buyer. I insert the word sometimes because if a trader wants to buy or sell and has patience, and the market is not quickly moving away, the trader can often buy for the bid price or sell at the offer price. In those instances where the trader may just want to jump in or out of the market right away, the trader would need to typically pay the offer or sell at the bid to fill the order immediately. Similar to fads that come and go with time, trading lingo sometimes changes, so be careful not to assume what used to be said then is still said now.

Trading natural gas can be as simple as calling your broker and buying or selling futures, or as complicated as buying physical at an index price, converting the index price into a NYMEX differential using a basis swap, buying futures to fix the price, taking delivery of the physical gas, transporting it to a storage facility and injecting it, withdrawing the gas at a later date, transporting it to a market area, and then selling it to an end user. There are hundreds of possible combinations of transactions which can be used to trade natural gas. The rest of this chapter covers the tools for hedging and trading natural gas, and provides real trading examples using them.

Futures

In April of 1990, the New York Mercantile Exchange (NYMEX) introduced and began trading a natural gas futures contract with the Henry Hub in Louisiana as a delivery location, and in August, 1995 the Kansas City Board of Trade (KCBT) introduced and began trading a Western natural gas futures contract with the Waha Hub in West Texas as a delivery point. The delivery points of these two contracts were chosen based on the high volume of trading activity and the high degree of volatility in price changes at the two points. The introduction of these futures contracts provided an efficient means of price discovery as well as new and exciting ways to trade natural gas.

Definition of Futures Contract

Futures are one of the many types of derivatives used in the financial markets for both commodities and securities. In terms of commodities such as natural gas, a futures contract is a tradable document which entitles the buyer of the contract to claim physical delivery of the commodity from the seller at the contract delivery point at a specified date in the future, and entitles the seller to deliver the physical commodity to the buyer under the same conditions. Because it is a tradable contract (can be bought and sold in an open market), its value changes as the supply of and demand for these contracts changes. As such, the value (price) of a futures contract is derived from the value (price) of the underlying commodity which it represents.

A common feature among all futures contracts is that they are standardized contracts. Each futures contract represents the same quantity and quality of the underlying physical commodity, valued in the same pricing format, to be delivered and received at the same delivery location. In addition, the date of delivery and receipt is the same for all contracts traded for a particular calendar month. The only element of a futures contract which can change when it is bought and sold is the price of the contract (the underlying commodity). By isolating the value of a futures contract in this way, market participants can utilize the contract for price discovery information, a hedging tool and a speculative investment vehicle.

Futures Contract Specifications

The standard contract specifications for the NYMEX natural gas futures contract are listed below:

Delivery Location:	Sabine Pipeline Hub at Henry, Louisiana
Contract Size:	1 contract equals 10,000 MMBtu
Minimum Price Change:	$0.001 per MMBtu (i.e., $10.00)
Maximum Price Change:	$0.75 for first two months, $0.15 all others
Number of Months Listed:	36 consecutive
Expiration Date:	3 business days prior to first of each contract month

The standard contract specifications for the KCBT Western natural gas futures contract are listed below:

Delivery Location:	Valero Pipeline Waha Hub in West Texas
Contract Size:	1 contract equals 10,000 MMBtu
Minimum Price Change:	$0.001 per MMBtu (i.e., $10.00) per contract
Maximum Price Change:	No limit in prompt contract, $0.10 - $0.15 all others
Number of Months Listed:	18 consecutive
Expiration Date:	2 business days prior to first of each contract month

Futures Trading Deadlines

The natural gas futures contracts are traded Monday through Friday except for major holidays when the exchanges are closed. The NYMEX natural gas futures contract begins trading at 9:00 a.m. Central time and closes at 2:10 p.m. Central time, regardless of whether it is expiration day or not. NYMEX natural gas futures contracts expire six business days prior to the beginning of each contract month. The KCBT Western natural gas futures contract begins trading at 8:30 a.m. Central time and closes at 2:30 p.m. Central time. KCBT Western natural gas futures contracts expire five business days prior to the beginning of each contract month. These deadlines and trading hours were established by the respective exchanges and are subject to modification as the exchange deems necessary.

Making and Taking Delivery

Not only can the natural gas futures contract be used for price discovery, a hedging tool, and a speculative investment vehicle, but it can also be used as a reliable source of supply and market. This is standard among all physical commodity futures markets. Anyone who has bought futures contracts and does not sell them before their expiration date must take delivery of the actual physical supply they have contracted to buy. In other words, the futures contracts will become physical obligations at expiration. This occurrence is called *taking delivery*. Conversely, anyone who has sold futures contracts short and does not buy them back before expiration will be required to supply that quantity of physical product for a buyer to receive. This is called *making delivery*.

Bi-Directional Trading

A unique feature of any futures market is the ability to enter long or short positions with equal ease. A long position is entered by buying, with the intention of either selling later at a higher price before expiration, or taking delivery of the physical at expiration. A short position is entered into by selling contracts with the intention of buying them back later at a lower price before expiration, or making delivery of the physical at expiration. This feature differs from shorting stocks or other securities wherein selling short requires borrowing the security from someone who owns it (long), selling it in the market, paying interest to a broker while the position is open, and then buying it back at a later date to return to the original holder. Futures traders enter into long positions to profit from rising prices, and enter into short positions to profit from falling prices.

Trading Futures on Margin

Another highlight of the futures markets is the enormous degree of leverage which can be obtained through the use of *margining*. As described above, leverage is the effect of magnifying the outcome of an investment through the use of borrowed funds, or a small down payment. In the futures market, this initial down payment is called margin. The *initial* margin requirement is the amount of money a trader must have on deposit with the exchange in order to buy or sell futures contracts.

In natural gas, for example, the current initial margin requirement for buying or selling one natural gas futures contract is roughly $3,000. (The initial margin requirement is set by the exchange and can change occasionally depending on several factors.) In other words, a trader needs only $3,000 in his or her account to buy or sell one futures contract, regardless of its outright value. If futures are trading $2.00, the initial margin requirement is only $3,000 for one contract instead of $20,000 (10,000 MMBtu at $2.00 = $20,000). This is leverage. It is for this reason that futures trading is considered to be extremely risky. A trader can control $20,000 worth of natural gas with one futures contract by putting up $3,000 of initial margin. If that futures contract price subsequently rises to $2.10 (which can happen in a matter of minutes), representing an outright value of $21,000 of natural gas, the futures trader can realize an astonishing 33 1/3 % return on a $3,000 investment, sometimes in only a matter of minutes! Leverage can also work against the trader, however. If futures prices had fallen to $1.90, the trader would have lost 33 1/3 % of the $3,000 investment. Instances such as this result in the issuance of a *margin maintenance call* by the futures exchange on a trader's account.

A trader will receive notice of a margin call if the value of its position has deteriorated beyond the amount of the initial margin requirement. That is, the futures exchange will require the trader to deposit additional funds into the account to cover this potential loss if it is realized. On the other hand, if an open position has appreciated in value beyond the initial margin requirement, the exchange will add funds to the futures account. So, for example, if the trader in the above example had paid $2.00 for one futures contract, posting $3,000 in initial margin, and the futures contract price subsequently fell below $1.70, the trader would be required to post additional margin by that amount. Consequently, if the futures contract price falls to $1.60, the trader would receive a margin maintenance call for $1,000. If the trader did not deposit the additional funds, the exchange would liquidate the position by selling the futures contract. (Margin requirements, other than initial, are calculated after the close of a trading day if an account has an open position.)

Other Characteristics of Futures

In the natural gas market, if a producer has supply at Henry Hub in Louisiana that it wishes to sell at a fixed price for the following month, it can now simply sell futures contracts instead of making phone calls to potential buyers as it did before. Once the short position has been entered, the producer can buy back and cover the position if prices fall or, after expiration, make delivery of the physical supply by not closing the position.

If the producer in the above example wants to make delivery by not buying back the futures contracts before expiration, there must be someone on the other side of the transaction wanting to take delivery. This is one reason commodity prices in general can be so volatile. For example, when the producer sells futures contracts, the first buyer may have no intention of taking delivery. If so, the contracts are sold to another trader who might also have no desire to take delivery. This process continues until the futures contracts end up in the possession of someone who does want to take delivery of the physical at expiration. Of course, prices can trade up and down during this entire process until expiration.

The majority of traders using the futures market to either speculate or hedge don't plan to make or take delivery of the physical product. At expiration, they liquidate any open positions by buying if they are short or selling if they are long. If there are more traders who are long with the intention of taking delivery of the physical gas after expiration than there are those who are short with the intention of making delivery to those buyers, the supply of available contracts at expiration is reduced. Therefore, anyone who is short and does not want to have to make delivery of the physical is forced to buy from a limited supply, thereby bidding up the price as they are trying to liquidate or close their open positions. The price will subsequently rise until it is high enough that some of those traders holding long positions feel the higher price is above their perceived value and consequently will sell out their long positions.

Another interesting phenomenon about any futures market is that there is always a zero sum gain at the expiration of a particular contract. No matter how much money some traders have made from buying and selling, it will be exactly offset by the same amount of money that other traders have lost from buying and selling. This is the case because, theoretically, the traders who made money did their trades with the traders who lost money. For example, if a futures market had only two participants, Bill and Ted, and Bill buys 10 futures contracts from Ted, Bill will make money if prices go up, and Ted will lose the same amount. The opposite is true if prices go down.

Prior to the natural gas futures contract, market participants relied on physical contracts between producers, end users, and trading companies to meet their fixed-price trading needs. These were very rigid markets in more ways than just price. For example, if an end user wanted to buy gas at the Henry Hub at a fixed price for the next three months, it may have taken several phone calls to find someone who would sell them the exact quantity they needed at the exact location and for the exact same time period they were looking for. The price was usually the easy part! The futures market is the solution to these difficulties. If the buyer in the above example needed 300,000 MMBtus per month in December, January, and February at Henry Hub, the buyer could simply buy 30 futures contracts in each month at the current market prices and take delivery of the physical gas at expiration.

Indexes

Definition

A frequently used pricing structure in the natural gas industry is an *index* price—a price which represents the most commonly traded fixed price at a major trading point during bid week. The indexes for several major trading points are published on the first day of each month by several industry newsletters which survey market participants for price information during bid week. The industry newsletter which is most commonly referenced is *Inside*

FERC Gas Market Report. (From this point forward, when the term index is used in this text,it refers to the index published by *Inside FERC Gas Market Report* for a specific trading point for that month.)

An index is typically identified first by pipeline, then by a producing or consuming region; a specific location, if there are several major trading points on that particular pipeline, such as the name of a meter station; a zone which corresponds to a pipeline's transportation rate structure; or a state where the pipeline originates, terminates, or passes through. For example, the February 1995 Index for Transco Zone 3 was $1.50, meaning that after bid week (the last week of January 1995), *Inside* FERC surveyed and posted $1.50 as the most commonly traded fixed price in Zone 3 for gas to flow the entire month of February, 1995. There are roughly 50 different indexes published by *Inside* FERC every month, each representing an individual location on the same or different pipelines.

Because the index for a specific trading point is theoretically the market value for that given month, many buyers and sellers will agree to transact at that price when it has been established. They agree during bid week that payment for the trade will be based on the index price, plus or minus any discount or premium the two parties negotiate. This form of pricing is common among producers because they prefer to sell most of their production at or above the market (index) each month and the rest at fixed prices which they think will be above index once it is published.

Value of Index Gas

The value of index gas varies depending on the location on a given pipeline or across different pipelines, and the particular time of the year. A trader might be willing to pay Kern River, Wyoming index plus $0.04 for gas at that location in January, but might only be willing to pay index minus $0.01 for the same gas in June. This is typically due to the differences in supply and demand fundamentals for a given month at a specific location. In addition, these premiums and discounts can change, similar to how fixed prices change, although the range in index values is not nearly as wide as that of fixed prices.

Buying and Selling Gas at Index

Prior to the end of bid week, profiting from trading natural gas at index prices is more difficult than at fixed prices because the index market is less volatile than the fixed-price market. This is because an index price is considered to be a *floating average* of fixed prices that are being traded during bid week. (*Inside* FERC determines the index price for a particular point as the mode price, not the true average or mean.)

For example, if the goal is to sell gas at a particular location at or above its monthly index, a trader could sell at index outright or sell at a fixed price that the trader speculates will be higher than index. By selling at index, the goal (but no more) will be achieved. But, by selling at a fixed price, achieving the goal depends on where that fixed price is relative to index when the index is published. If prices rise for the remainder of bid week after making the sale, index will most likely be above the fixed sale price. If prices fall for the remainder of bid-week, index will most likely be below the fixed sale price. The fixed-price sale alternative is more risky (in terms of reaching the stated goal), but could be more rewarding.

The situation in the example above is very real for many market participants. In the case of producers, some of their traders are provided with incentive bonus plans based on how much above index they are able to sell the company's production. As a measure of prudence, utilities often gauge their procurement costs for supply in terms of how close the supply cost is to a particular index or basket of indices. Marketing companies have a similar interest in index pricing, but for the purposes of risk management instead of as a benchmark.

Index vs. Fixed-price Trading

The difference in volatility between index pricing and fixed pricing contributes to the importance of index pricing as a risk management tool. (Index pricing is the pricing structure which has the lowest volatility and, therefore, risk.) This difference can be substantial depending on the overall volatility in prices for the natural gas market. In a particular region during bid week, for example, the range of index-priced trades might be from index plus $0.01, to index plus $0.05, allowing for a maximum profit or loss of $0.04 by buying the low and selling the high. In contrast, the range of fixed-price trades could be as wide as $1.75 to $2.25, representing a $0.50 profit or loss possibility.

Trading opportunities exist, therefore, based on the degree of risk a company is willing to take in order to make an expected return. For marketing companies interested in a low-risk approach to trading, the most ideal opportunity would be one in which they could buy gas at index (or a discount to index) and sell it at index plus a premium. Although this "premium" or "discount" is a purely negotiated number between the parties involved, the market for index gas is so transparent (liquid) that being able to buy and sell gas outright in terms of index, and then make a profit, proves to be nearly impossible at times. Traders will find that arbitrage opportunities rarely exist in the index market because of its transparency and lack of volatility. For that reason, companies wishing to take higher risk, in order to make an expected higher return, try to time the market by trading gas at fixed prices, hoping to catch the high or the low in the cycle. The approach which falls in the middle of the risk spectrum is the combination of both pricing methods. By buying gas at an index price and selling it at a fixed price, or by buying gas at a fixed price and selling it at an index price, the volatility in the trade is lessened because the index price is changing at a slower rate than fixed prices are. This trading approach, albeit less risky than fixed-price trading, still carries a significant

amount of risk. This fixed price versus floating (index) price risk can be hedged with the use of a risk management tool known as a swap.

Swaps

Definition

In the most generic sense possible, a swap can be most simply defined as an agreement between two parties to exchange, at some future point, one product, either physical or financial, for another.

Physical Natural Gas Swap

As an example of a physical swap in the natural gas market, let's suppose a trader has an opportunity to sell gas in Louisiana next month. Making phone calls to several producers with supply in Louisiana, the trader finds only one seller. The seller however, won't sell his supply in Louisiana unless the trader agrees to sell him the same amount of gas in West Texas so he can supply a new industrial customer. During numerous phone calls in trying to find Louisiana supply, the trader inadvertently discovered a seller of West Texas gas! So, the trader proposes a physical swap with the Louisiana seller. The producer agrees, and the trader calls the person with West Texas supply and buys the gas for the following month. The trader then transfers it to the Louisiana seller (the swap counterparty) and, in return, receives supply in Louisiana. This is a simplified example of a physical swap in the natural gas market.

Financial Swaps Defined

A financial swap is another type of derivative which obtains its value from the price or prices of one or more financial products, such as an index or a futures contract. A financial swap involves the exchange of payments between two parties, one of which is negotiated and set at a known price (fixed) at the time the swap is entered into, the other of which is established by an unbiased third party (floating) at some mutually agreed upon future point in time (Fig 4.1).

At the time the swap is entered into, the two payments are considered to be of equal value.

Fig. 4.1 Generic Swap

Through the use of swaps, natural gas traders can convert one form of pricing into another, thereby eliminating the discrepancies between different pricing structures. This is accomplished by exchanging (swapping) with another party the cash flow from one form of pricing for the cash flow of another. For example, if a trading company is buying gas at a fixed price and selling it at a floating price, it can swap the fixed price for a floating price, or vice versa, with a party that has the opposite risk, thereby hedging the exposure. The swap which accomplishes this task is appropriately called a *fixed-for-floating* swap.

Buying vs. Selling Fixed-For-Floating Swaps

In order to differentiate between which party is the buyer of a fixed-float swap and which party is the seller, a standard has been adopted which essentially determines the direction of the trade for each party based on which direction the fixed-price cash flow component of the swap is going.

Buyer of Fixed-Float Swap. The Buyer of any type of fixed-float swap in the natural gas market pays a fixed price to the other party and receives a floating price from that party.

Seller of Fixed-Float Swap. The Seller of any type of fixed-float swap in the natural gas market receives a fixed price from the other party and pays a floating price to that party. There are four types of fixed-float swaps used in the natural gas market. The most common is a fixed-float *futures swap*, followed by (with a slight variation) B*asis Swaps*, the combination of fixed-float futures swaps and basis swaps called fixed-float *index swaps*, and finally fixed-float *swing swaps*. Each type of swap plays an important role in managing the different risks inherent in most natural gas trades.

Futures Look-Alike Swaps

One of the most actively traded natural gas fixed-float swaps, are futures look-alike swaps (hereafter referred to as a fixed-float futures swaps or simply futures swaps.) This type of swap performs almost the same function as a futures contract with the exception that, after expiration of the futures contract, there is a financial settlement for futures swaps (exchange of payments), as opposed to a physical settlement (making or taking delivery if an open position is held through expiration) in the case of actual futures contracts.

Comparing Futures Swaps and Futures Contracts

Price discovery in the futures market is as easy as looking at the latest posted (traded) price on the futures quote screen. Discovering value in the futures swap market is theoretically the latest futures price, but must be obtained through the OTC market. This is because execution (trading) of fixed-float futures swaps is done in the OTC market, but if each trader involved in the transaction knows where the actual futures market is trading, the use of an OTC broker is to simply match two interested parties.

Futures swaps and futures contracts have the same two basic components—a fixed price and a floating price. The fixed price of a futures contract is what the contract is worth in the market for that particular month at that particular moment in time. The fixed price for futures swaps is theoretically the same as the current futures contract price for that particular month, as its intended purpose is to track the value of that contract. The difference in the floating-price component between actual futures contracts and fixed-float futures swaps is that the floating price of the futures contract is the current price, the price at which the contracts are bought or sold before expiration, or the final settlement price on expiration day if making or taking delivery of the physical natural gas. The floating price in futures swaps is a calculated price, most commonly known in the industry as the **L3D Price** for that contract month.

The L3D Price Defined

At the time of this writing, the "simple average of the last three trading day's futures settlement prices" (hereafter referred to as simply, L3D) is the standard floating price of all futures swaps. The *settlement price* for any given trading day, is calculated by the futures exchange as the true weighted-average price of every trade done in the final two minutes of trading for that day. On the last trading day, the settlement price is calculated by the futures exchange as the true weighted-average of every trade done during the final 30 minutes of trading for that day except on the last trading day for a contract. Settlement prices are final and appear in newspapers and other publications each day. Therefore, the L3D is the simple average of these final settlement prices for the last three trading days of a given contract month. (e.g., If the Nov. futures contract expiration date, or last trading day, is October 22, the L3D would be the simple average of the futures settlement prices on October 20, 21, and 22, assuming they were business days.) This floating price was chosen based on a consensus agreement between traders that using the **L3D** would be less volatile (similar to an index) than using only the last day's closing price. However, many futures swaps are traded with a last day settlement price as the floating price due to specific pricing structures in physical trades, or because the swap is transacted in the last three days of trading.

Mechanics of Futures Swaps

The mechanics of a futures swap are simple. The buyer pays a fixed price and in return receives the L3D for that contract month from the seller. As such, futures swaps are very frequently used in place of actual futures contracts because the effect of a change in the fixed price of the swap (which would be caused by a change in the price of the underlying futures contract) result in the same immediate outcome as if futures contracts had been bought or sold instead. In addition, the L3D corresponds to the floating price of other types of swaps and also functions as an alternate pricing method for physical gas. Furthermore, although rarely the case, some companies don't have actual futures trading accounts set up with the futures exchanges and futures swaps provide them with a way to participate in the price action of the futures market.

Example of a Basic Futures Swap Trade

In a basic fixed-float futures swap, FJS buys a Dec. futures swap from XYZ, wherein FJS pays a fixed price of $2.00 to XYZ, and XYZ pays the Dec. L3D to FJS. The outcome of the swap for FJS is simple. FJS will profit if L3D is greater than $2.00, FJS will break-even if L3D equals $2.00, or FJS will lose money if L3D is less than $2.00.

The net result of the above example is also very similar to the outcomes possible if FJS instead pays $2.00 for futures contracts. The difference is that by using futures contracts, FJS can wait until the last day at the last minute to sell, or at any time during trading day hours between now and then. Futures swaps, since they are actually traded OTC, are actively trading both before and during trading hours, and after the futures markets close. However, because the futures swap market is very active and liquid, FJS could turn around and sell the swap at any time to any other party before the third-to-last trading day of futures. Furthermore, some traders will even allow the floating price of futures swaps to be modified to be just the last day's futures settlement price. Depending on the trader, this modification could cost more for the party making the request in terms of either paying a higher fixed price (when buying) or receiving a lower fixed price (when selling) had it been a standard L3D floating price.

Other Applications of Futures Swaps

Fixed-float futures swaps are useful in situations other than simply speculating on the price direction of the futures market. Pricing structures for physical gas transactions and other swaps often reference L3D in some form or another. For example, a producer might want to sell some gas at fixed prices, some at index prices, and some at L3D prices. Because physical trades at L3D share the common floating price, futures swaps are used to manage that floating price risk.

Hedging Futures Swaps with Futures Contracts

Because futures swaps are traded in much the same way actual futures contracts are, many trading companies are in the business of just trading futures swaps and hedging them with futures contracts, never intending to trade the physical natural gas. These companies, such as hedge funds, banks, and large independent traders, make money by selling futures swaps at a premium to futures or buying futures swaps at a discount to futures, and skillfully liquidating their futures position (if any) before expiration of that months futures contract.

Let's suppose Eric, a natural gas futures trader, is responsible for trading futures swaps for a bank (no physical trading capability) to make a profit. Believe it or not, Eric doesn't need much knowledge about the physical natural gas market in order to do his job successfully. For example, suppose a customer calls the company during the trading day and wants to buy 10,000 MMBtu/d of April fixed-float futures swaps. Eric immediately calls his futures broker on a special direct phone line, keeping the customer on the other phone, and asks for the April market. The broker gives him a $2.25 bid at $2.255 market for April, and Eric relays his offer price to sell 10,000 MMBtu/d of April fixed-float futures swaps at $2.26 to his customer on the other phone. The customer needs to hedge a just-completed deal, and because $2.26 is a good hedge price, the customer agrees to pay $2.26, and in return receive L3D April. Therefore, Eric needs to buy 30 April futures contracts because he has sold a total of 30 contract equivalents as a swap (One contract = 10,000 MMBtu, and One contract per day for 30 days = 30 total contracts.) He quickly gives his futures broker an order to, "Pay $2.255 or better for 30 April." The broker executes the trade and pays $2.255 for 30 April futures contracts. Now what? Figure 4.2 illustrates the transaction up to this point.

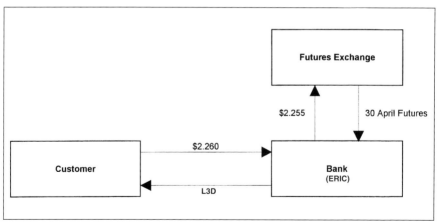

Fig.4.2 Hedging Futures Swap Purchases with Futures Contracts

Although Eric is not exposed to any fixed-price risk once the trade is done, he does have two positions to contend with. Under the futures swap, Eric will receive $2.26 from his customer, but must pay them L3D April in return. In addition, Eric now has 30 April futures contracts in his account which he must sell before the April contract expires. If he doesn't liquidate the position, his company will be required by the exchange to take delivery of the physical gas, which they can't do as they are not in the physical trading business.

Trading Out of a Futures Swap Hedged with Futures Contracts

Because he has sold a futures swap and hedged it with futures contracts, Eric needs L3D April to pay to his customer, and must sell his futures. There are two methods he can use to accomplish this task—buy a futures swap and sell his futures contracts, or sell his futures contracts at a price which equals L3D. Let's go through each method.

Unwinding is the term used in the swap market for the process whereby a position or positions, created from a previous swap trade or series of swap trades, is eliminated by entering trades in the equal and opposite direction of the previous trade.

Continuing the example above, the safest and easiest way for Eric to receive L3D April and sell his futures contracts is to reverse, or unwind, the original transaction. Let's suppose that another customer calls Eric the following day and wants to sell 10,000 MMBtu/d of April fixed-float futures swaps, and asks for Eric's bid. Again, Eric immediately calls his futures broker and asks for the April market. The broker gives him a $2.30 bid at $2.32 market for April, and Eric relays his bid price of $2.305 for 10,000 MMBtu/d of April fixed-float futures swaps to his customer on the other phone. This customer also needs to hedge a just-completed deal, and they agree to sell at $2.305, and in return pay L3D April. As a result, Eric needs to sell 30 April futures contracts because he bought a total of 30 contract equivalents as a swap, he quickly gives his futures broker an order to, "Sell 30 April at $2.305 or better." The broker executes the trade and actually does better by selling 30 April futures contracts at $2.31. Now that this trade is done, effectively unwinding the previous trade, Eric can count his money. Figure 4.3 illustrates what the two transactions look like together and the schedule of payments and receipts that follow show the total profit/loss for the two trades. Dotted lines represent futures contracts, not physical gas.

Receive from 1st swap (+)	$2.26
Pay to 1st swap (-)	L3D
Receive from 2nd swap (+)	L3D
Pay to 2nd swap (-)	$2.305
Futures bought (-)	$2.255
Futures sold (+)	$2.310

Profit/loss on trade + $0.01 per contract x 30 contracts = $3,000

Liquidating, in terms of a commodity or security, is the process whereby a futures position created from a previous trade or series of trades is eliminated by buying or selling the futures contracts in the equal and opposite direction of the position.

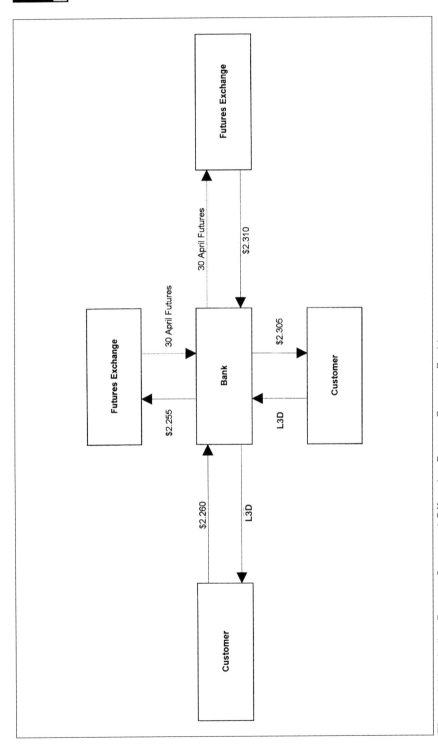

Fig. 4.3 Unwinding Futures Swap and Offsetting Futures Contract Position

The other way for Eric to liquidate is not quite as safe nor as easy. Assuming he hasn't been able to unwind the original futures swap by selling another futures swap, Eric is faced with the difficult task of selling his futures contracts at a price equal to or better than (higher) L3D April. He can do this one of two ways. He can speculate by selling them before the last three trading day period at a price he thinks will be equal to or better than L3D or he can sell one-third of his futures contracts on each of the last three trading days of the settlement period, thereby attempting to replicate L3D April. The first alternative needs no explanation, just some expert forecasting abilities and lots of luck! The second alternative however, is the most common method of liquidating futures contracts, aside from unwinding the position with another futures swap.

From the sound of it, liquidating one-third of the total futures position on each of the last three trading days by trying to buy or sell at their respective settlement prices seems like a nearly impossible task. First, the settlement price (the true weighted-average price of all trades done during the settlement period) for a given trading day isn't even posted until nearly 45 minutes after the market has closed for the day. Second, how does a trader know how much volume is being traded at each price during the settlement period to even give him or her a feel for what the settlement price might be? And third, how does a trader know when to buy or sell (depending on his or her position) during the settlement period? This confusion is known as *liquidation risk*. Liquidation risk is the risk that a trader cannot successfully eliminate his or her open futures position at a price exactly equal to L3D. Again, this risk can and should always be hedged by unwinding the L3D exposure with futures swaps, but, if this can't be done at a reasonable price, the liquidation risk has to be dealt with.

Helpful Hints for Liquidating Futures

a   Break down the number of contracts which you need to buy or sell on a given day into an equal number of groups. For example, 100 / 4 = 4 groups of 25 contracts each.

b   Break down the time frame which covers the settlement period for that day into the same number of periods as you have groups. For example, two minutes / 4 = 4 periods of 30 seconds each, or 30 minutes / 4 = 4 periods of 7.5 minutes each.

c   Buy or sell (depending on the open position) one group during each time period, no matter what the market is doing at that time.

d   Keep your fingers crossed that your final average price comes out close to the final futures settlement price!

As a general rule, the more groups you can break your total position into for a given day, the better. However, keep in mind that you are going to have to break the given settlement time frame into the same number of groups, and that you wouldn't realistically benefit much more by buying or selling one contract every second for 30 minutes than by buying or selling 120 every two minutes. Besides, your futures broker would probably laugh and hang up on you if you gave an order to buy or sell one contract at the market every second for half an hour!

Example of Hedging a Physical Trade with a Futures Swap

Let's suppose that during October (Oct.), FJS trading company has sold gas to a market at Henry Hub in Louisiana for the month of November (Nov.) with this pricing structure:Price = L3D Nov. + $0.02.

The sale price will be calculated as the average of the last three day's settlement prices for the November futures contract plus a $0.02 / MMBtu premium. As a result, FJS has made a physical sale for Nov. at a floating price (L3D + $0.02), which it must buy physical supply for by the end of Nov bidweek. For the purposes of demonstrating the use of a fixed-float futures swap, we will assume FJS is going to buy physical gas at a fixed price at Henry to supply this market. Figure 4.4 illustrates the initial deal structure up to this point.

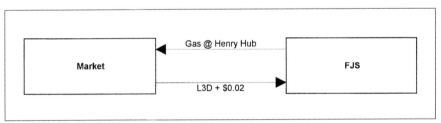

Figure 4.4 Physical Sale at Floating Price to Futures

Assuming FJS is going to buy physical gas at a fixed price at Henry to cover the physical sale it has made at L3D + $0.02, FJS will use a fixed-float futures swap to determine what fixed price it can pay to a supplier, hedge the floating price risk, and lock in a profit on the trade. Since FJS will be receiving, and therefore possess, this floating price (L3D + $0.02) from the market, and will need a fixed price to pay a supplier, FJS is a seller of the futures swap (i.e., receives fixed price and pays L3D.)

How does FJS determine the fixed price it can pay a supplier? It simply depends on what fixed price the futures swap buyer will pay. So, how does FJS know what the fixed price of the fixed-float futures swap is? If you recall, this type of swap is a futures look-alike, and theoretically has the same value as the futures contract for the pertaining month. Therefore, even though executing the trade requires FJS to go into the OTC market to find a party interested in doing the trade, FJS relies on its futures quote screen to provide the approximate fixed-price in the futures swap market.

The incomplete schedule of payments and receipts below illustrates the relationship between what the futures swap buyer will pay and what FJS can pay to its supplier.

Receive from market (+)	L3D + $0.02
Pay to swap (-)	L3D
Receive from swap (+)	X
Pay to supplier (-)	Y
Profit / loss on trade	(X − Y) + $0.02

The fixed price which will be received from the swap buyer is represented by the letter X and the fixed price to be paid to the supplier is represented by the letter Y because we are trying to solve for them or, more specifically, the relationship between them. Avoiding a long algebraic problem-solving mission, it should be fairly clear that the trade will break-even if $X − Y = −\$0.02$, be profitable if $X − Y > −\$0.02$, or lose money if $X − Y < −\$0.03$. In other words, substituting for X and Y, this trade will be break-even if FJS pays $0.02 more for fixed-price physical gas at Henry than the fixed price it can receive from the futures swap counterparty at that point in time. For example, if the futures screen is at $1.90. FJS can afford to pay up to $1.92 for fixed-price physical gas at Henry. Therefore, FJS can pay up to $0.02 more than the futures screen price at that moment for the gas, no matter what price it shows, and FJS will break-even on the trade. In completing the circle then, the sales price to the market is essentially floating at the futures screen price + $0.02. Figure 4.5 and the schedule of payments and receipts illustrate this trade and show the calculated result based on receiving $1.90 from the futures swap counterparty, and paying $1.91 to a supplier for physical gas at Henry.

Receive from market (+)	L3D + $0.02
Pay to swap (−)	L3D
Receive from swap (+)	$1.90
Pay to supplier (−)	$1.91
Profit / loss on trade	+$0.01 per MMBtu x 300,000 MMBtu = $3,000

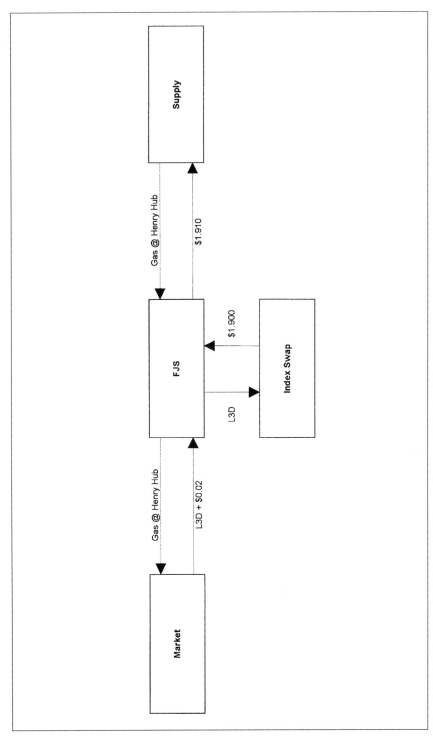

Fig. 4.5 Hedging Physical Sale with Futures Swap and Physical Purchase

Example of Hedging a Physical Trade with Futures

Let's look at how FJS Trading Company in the earlier example could have used futures contracts instead of a futures swap to hedge its physical trade.

To demonstrate the use of futures contracts to hedge this transaction, we will again assume FJS is going to buy physical gas at a fixed price at Henry. FJS is in a situation where it receives L3D + $0.02 from the market and pays a fixed-price to a supplier. Instead of selling a fixed-float futures swap (receive fixed price, pay L3D), FJS will sell futures contracts at a fixed price and buy those futures contracts back at a price equal to L3D (thereby paying L3D). FJS must liquidate (buy) those futures during the last three trading days by paying the L3D price or better (lower). So, where FJS previously depended on the fixed price a futures swap buyer would pay, the fixed price it can receive from selling futures now determines what fixed price it can pay a supplier.

By substituting "pay to swap" with "futures bought," and by substituting "receive from swap" with "futures sold," the incomplete schedule of payments and receipts following expresses the same relationship between the fixed price FJS can pay its supplier and the fixed price it receives from selling futures.

Receive from market (+)	L3D + $0.02
Futures bought (−)	L3D
Futures sold (+)	X
Pay to supplier (−)	Y
Profit / loss on trade	(X − Y) + $0.02

The relationship between the price at which FJS can sell futures and the price which FJS can pay its supplier for physical fixed-price gas at Henry is identical to the earlier example: This trade will be at least break-even if FJS pays no more than $0.02 more for fixed-price physical gas at Henry than the fixed price they can receive from selling futures contracts at that point in time.

For example, a customer wants to sell physical fixed-price gas to FJS at Henry at $2.35 and futures are $2.35 bid at $2.36. FJS will buy 10,000 MMBtu/d of physical gas at $2.35 and simultaneously sell 30 futures contracts at $2.35. That's the easy part. The difficult part is the liquidation. Assuming FJS is successful at liquidating 30 futures at L3D, Figure 4.6 and the following completed schedule of payments and receipts will illustrate the finished transaction and total profit/loss for the trade.

Receive from market (+)	L3D + $0.02
Futures bought (−)	L3D
Futures sold (+)	$2.35
Pay to supplier (−)	$2.35
Profit / loss on trade	+$0.02 per contract x 30 contracts = $6,000

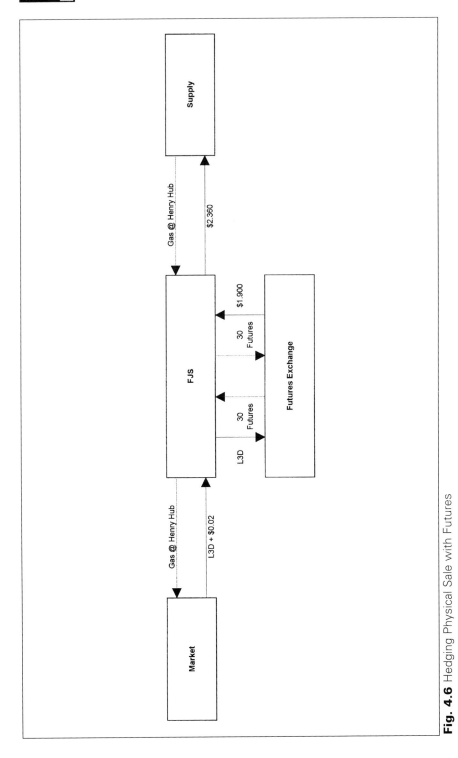

Fig. 4.6 Hedging Physical Sale with Futures

FJS could have hedged its liquidation risk before the third-to-last futures trading day by selling a fixed-float futures swap and simultaneously buying back the futures.

Futures Swaps vs. Futures Contracts for Hedging Trades

Because futures swap traders, such as in the example above, are constantly trying to *scalp* (buy futures swaps at a discount to futures, and sell them at a premium), using actual futures contracts to hedge positions is usually more economical in terms of time and money. If a company has done a fixed-price trade that it wants to hedge with a futures swap, it would have to either call several futures swap traders to find someone to transact with, or pay an OTC broker to find another party. In addition, the price that the swap party is willing to transact for will most likely not be as good as the current bid or offer in the futures market because that counterparty needs to be compensated for the unwind, or liquidation, risk after doing the trade. However, in those trades where the pricing structure references an L3D price, the safest hedge is a futures swap. Consequently, a good argument exists for using both tools to hedge trades where applicable.

Fixed-price physical trades at locations other than a futures contract delivery point can be hedged against the same fixed-price changes. Trades such as these are still hedged using futures swaps and futures contracts, but contain another risk which can, and should, be hedged using another type of natural gas swap called a basis swap.

Basis Swaps
Definition of Basis

B*asis*, in the natural gas market, is the difference in value between gas at one delivery point and gas at another. The standard reference when calculating a basis differential for gas at another location is the delivery point for a natural gas futures contract, either NYMEX or KCBT. (For the remainder of this chapter, unless otherwise noted, reference will be made only to NYMEX for the purpose of simplicity.) For example, if the May Henry Hub index is $2.25 and the May EPNG Permian index is $1.75, the actual basis differential for May Permian is minus $0.50 to Henry. (The basis differential for a particular location is made in reference to the futures contract delivery point, not the futures contract delivery point to the particular location. Hence, Permian is minus $0.50 to Henry.)

As opposed to the actual basis differential, which is a known number, there is what is sometimes called the forward basis differential, which is a forecast of what the actual basis differential will be. This concept is similar to the forward fixed-price market for natural gas, or more commonly known as the futures market. Since the Henry Hub index for any month beyond the current month is unknown, the point of reference for a forward basis differential is the corresponding futures contract. As such, there is an actively traded market for forward basis differentials. This market is more commonly known as the *basis swap* market.

The basis swap market is where traders forecast the actual basis differential for a particular index as they buy and sell basis swaps, just as futures traders are trying to forecast the fixed price of gas at Henry Hub at expiration of a contract month as they buy and sell futures. Basis swaps are traded in the OTC market and require constant attention, via phone calls to other traders or OTC brokers, to maintain current quotes. Although not quite as active as the futures market or the physical cash market, the basis swap market is extremely active at certain times.

Mechanics of a Basis Swap

Basis swaps are derivatives, and as such, are priced based on the prices of, in this case, two underlying financial products—an index price and a futures contract price. The mechanics of a basis swap are not quite as straightforward as a futures swap, but are similar. The buyer makes a fixed-price payment to the seller and receives a floating payment from that party in return. The floating price component is the index for a particular location. The fixed price, however, is not really a fixed price but rather is the L3D price for the particular month, plus or minus a fixed basis differential. In effect, the only part of the fixed-price that is fixed at the time the swap is traded is the basis differential. The other part is the L3D price for that month. How can this work? How useful is a swap if you are paying a floating price and receiving a different floating price, plus or minus a basis differential? Refer to Figure 4.7 for an illustration of how the cash flows in a basis swap are exchanged, assuming the buyer pays L3D minus $0.25 and receives Permian index.

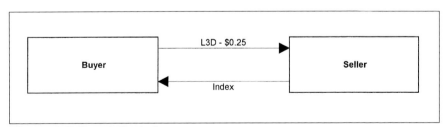

Figure 4.7 Generic Basis Swap

The following schedule will help determine the profit/loss parameters for the buyer in this transaction.

Receive from swap (+)	Index
Pay to swap (−)	L3D − $0.25

Profit on trade where:	(L3D − $0.25) < Index
Lose on trade where:	(L3D − $0.25) > Index

Through simple algebraic manipulation, the above parameters could be written:

Profit on trade where:	(Index − L3D) > − $0.25
Lose on trade where:	(Index − L3D) < − $0.25

This is the standard pricing format when referring to basis differentials. For example, Permian trades at a negative basis differential to futures. However, there are locations which trade at a positive basis differential to futures, such as CGT Appalachia, and these are quoted accordingly. Therefore, if the actual basis differential of April EPNG Permian index to L3D April futures is greater than minus $0.25 or less than minus $0.25, FJS will make money or lose money, respectively. minus $0.20 is greater than minus $0.25, and minus $0.30 is less than minus $0.25, but basis swap traders will refer to minus $0.20 as tighter and minus $0.30 as wider to avoid the confusion.

Applications for Basis Swaps

Basis swaps are embedded within fixed-float index swaps forward fixed-price physical gas (not futures), and exchange of futures for physical (EFP) transactions. Therefore, basis swaps are used by almost everyone in the natural gas market in some way or another.

Price Discovery. From a broader perspective, basis swaps are the means by which value in the coming months for natural gas at locations other than the futures contract delivery point is discovered. Given the current futures price for a particular month at a point in time, and by adjusting that price by the current basis differential for a location which has a corresponding index published for it, the fixed price value of gas at that location can be determined for that particular month at that point in time.

Risk Management. In addition to a price discovery tool, many market participants use basis swaps to manage their basis risk. Basis risk can be most easily defined as the risk that a given change in the price of gas in one location (specifically a futures contract delivery point) will not be reflected in a corresponding change of equal magnitude and direction in another location. For example, using the futures contract as a price reference for Henry Hub, if futures rise by $0.10, but prices at Permian rise by only $0.09, this represents slight basis risk. Similarly, if futures fall by $0.10, but prices at Permian rise by

$0.05, this represents extreme basis risk in that there is little or no correlation between prices in Permian and futures prices. Therefore, any party which enters into a fixed-price physical transaction at any location other than a futures contract delivery point, and subsequently enters into a futures swap or uses the actual futures contracts to hedge that fixed-price risk, is exposed to basis risk and can use a basis swap to manage that risk. The following example will help illustrate this point.

Hedging Fixed-Price Sale
at Alternate Delivery Location

Let's suppose FJS trading company has sold 10,000 MMBtu/d of physical gas for April on EPNG Permian Basin at $1.75 and it has bought the same volume of physical gas for April at the same location at Permian index to supply the sale. The risk to FJS at this point is clear. If prices rise and index is greater than $1.75, FJS will lose money, but if prices fall and index is less than $1.75, FJS will make money. After examining its risk up to this point, FJS decides that, as a hedge against prices rising, it will pay the current market price ($2.05) for 30 futures contracts (equivalent to 300,000 MMBtu). FJS knows that if futures prices rise, it will make money in its futures account which it assumes will be enough to offset what it will lose on the physical sale in Permian at $1.75. If prices fall, FJS knows it will lose money in its futures account, but assumes the gain from its short sale in Permian at $1.75 will be enough to offset the loss. This sounds like a logical hedge, but is full of risk, all of which can be reduced, through an additional hedge using a basis swap. Refer to Figure 4.8a which illustrates the structure of the transaction up to this point, assuming FJS liquidates the 30 April futures contracts at L3D April.

Let's look at an incomplete schedule of payments and receipts for FJS under this transaction to try and define the parameter prices within which FJS will profit or lose on the trade.

Receive from market (+)	$1.75
Futures bought (−)	$2.05
Futures sold (+)	L3D
Pay to supplier (−)	Index

Profit on trade where:	(L3D − Index) > $0.30
Lose on trade where:	(L3D − Index) < $0.30

Through simple algebraic manipulation, the above parameters could be written:

Profit on trade where:	(Index − L3D) < − $0.30
Lose on trade where:	(Index − L3D) > − $0.30

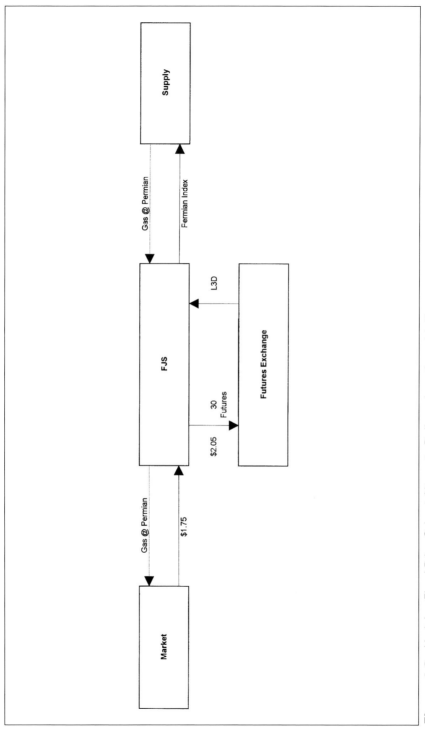

Figure 4.8a Hedging Fixed-Price Sale at Alternate Delivery Location with Futures

After calculating the profit/loss parameters, it should be clear that FJS has basis risk in this transaction. That is, when index and L3D become known, if the actual basis differential is wider than minus $0.30 (e.g., minus $0.40), FJS will profit. If the actual basis differential is tighter than minus $0.30 (e.g., minus $0.20), FJS will lose money.

In keeping with good risk management practices, therefore, FJS decides to enter into a basis swap to hedge the basis risk in its fixed-price physical sale in the Permian. Should FJS buy or sell the basis swap, and at what differential should the trade be done? The answer to the first part of the question is simple—since FJS is going to receive L3D when it liquidates the April futures, it should buy the basis swap, wherein FJS pays L3D plus or minus some basis differential and receives Permian Index. This is the proper direction of the trade for two reasons. First, FJS will pass through the L3D price it receives, and second, FJS will profit from the basis swap if the actual basis differential tightens from the differential it negotiates with the basis swap seller. The differential FJS should therefore try to buy from the basis swap seller should be wider than minus $0.30 for it to make a profit on the trade. Again, this basis differential comes from the schedule of payments and receipts, and marks the break-even point for FJS in terms of where the actual basis differential is when it becomes known.

Let's assume that FJS is able to pay L3D minus $0.35 for an April Permian basis swap to XYZ basis trader, and in return receive Permian index from XYZ. The diagram from above now includes the basis swap transaction (Fig. 4.8b). The completed schedule of payments and receipts calculates the net profit for the trade.

Receive from market (+)	$1.75
Futures bought (−)	$2.05
Futures sold (+)	L3D
Pay to basis swap (−)	L3D − $0.35
Receive from basis swap (+)	Index
Pay to supplier (−)	Index

Profit on trade: $0.05 x 30 contracts = $15,000

As you can see from the diagram and schedule of payments and receipts, FJS has completely hedged both the fixed-price risk,and the basis risk. Regardless of where futures prices or Permian prices go, the end-result of the trade will be a $0.05 per MMBtu profit (or $15,000) for FJS. A fixed-float futures swap can always be used in place of trading actual futures contracts. This particular example, and other trades where the L3D price is a component of the trade, demonstrates how the use of a futures swap could be a more efficient hedge in that it eliminates liquidation risk at expiration. The following table below confirms the outcome of this trade as it shows various price assumptions for April Permian index and L3D April:

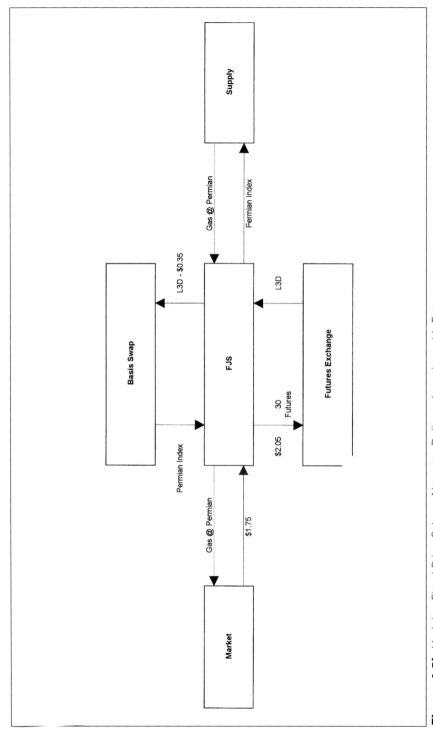

Figure 4.8b Hedging Fixed-Price Sale at Alternate Delivery Location with Futures

Index	FJS rec.'s L3D	Futures from Mkt.	Futures Bought	Pay to Sold	Rec. from Basis Swap	Pay to Basis Swap	Total Supplier	Net Profit/(Loss)
A $2.05	$1.45	$1.75	$2.05	$1.45	$1.10	$2.05	$2.05	$15,000
B $1.75	$1.75	$1.75	$2.05	$1.75	$1.40	$1.75	$1.75	$15,000
C $1.45	$2.05	$1.75	$2.05	$1.75	$1.70	$1.45	$1.45	$15,000

Hedging Fixed-Price Purchase at Alternate Delivery Location

The next example is the opposite transaction of that in the previous example. All price assumptions are the same except for the differential in the basis swap trade.

Let's suppose FJS trading company has paid $1.75 for 10,000 MMBtu/d of physical gas for April on EPNG at Permian Basin, and it has sold the same volume of physical gas for April at the same location at Permian index. The risk to FJS at this point is clear. If prices fall and index is consequently less than $1.75, FJS will lose money. If prices rise and Index is consequently greater than $1.75, FJS will make money.

After examining its risk up to this point, FJS decides that, as a hedge against falling prices, it will sell 30 futures at the current market price ($2.05). FJS knows that if futures prices rise it will lose money in its futures account, but assumes the gain from its purchase in Permian at $1.75 will be enough to offset the loss. If prices fall, FJS knows it will make money in its futures account which it assumes will be enough to offset what it will lose on the $1.75 purchase it has made in Permian. This sounds like a logical hedge, but is full of risk, all of which can be eliminated through an additional hedge using a basis swap. Refer to Figure 4.9a which illustrates the structure of the transaction up to this point:

Let's look at an incomplete schedule of payments and receipts for FJS under this transaction to try and define the parameter prices within which FJS will profit or lose on the trade assuming FJS liquidates the 30 April futures contracts at L3D April.

Pay to supplier (−)	$1.75
Futures sold (+)	$2.05
Futures bought (−)	L3D
Receive from market (+)	Index

Profit on trade where:	(L3D − Index) < $0.30
Lose on trade where:	(L3D − Index) > $0.30

Through simple algebraic manipulation, the above parameters could be written:

Profit on trade where:	(Index − L3D) > − $0.30
Lose on trade where:	(Index − L3D) < − $0.30

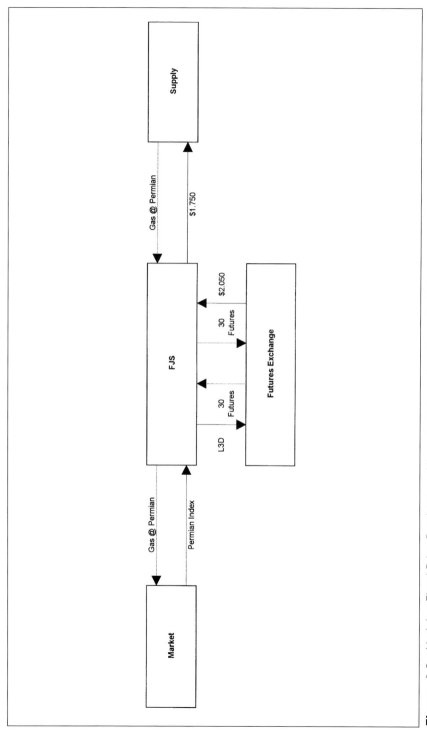

Figure 4.9a Hedging Fixed-Price Purchase at Alternate Delivery Location with Futures

After calculating the profit/loss parameters, it should be clear that FJS has basis risk in this transaction. That is, when index and L3D are established, if the actual basis differential is tighter than minus $0.30, FJS will profit. If the actual basis differential is wider than minus $0.30, FJS will lose money.

In keeping with good risk management practices, FJS decides to enter into a basis swap to hedge the basis risk in its fixed-price physical purchase. Should FJS buy or sell the basis swap, and at what differential should the trade be done? The answer to the first part of the question is simple. Since FJS is going to pay L3D when it liquidates the April futures, it should sell the basis swap, wherein FJS receives L3D plus or minus some basis differential and pays Permian index. This is the proper direction of the trade for two reasons—FJS will pass through the index price it receives, and FJS will profit from the basis swap if the actual basis differential widens from the differential it negotiates with the basis swap buyer. The differential that FJS should therefore sell to the basis swap buyer should be tighter than minus $0.30 for it to make a profit on the trade.

Let's assume that FJS is able to sell an April Permian basis swap to XYZ basis trader at L3D minus $0.25. The diagram for this transaction is Figure 4.9b. The completed schedule of payments and receipts which follows calculates the net profit for the trade.

Pay to supplier (−)	$1.75
Futures sold (+)	$2.05
Futures bought (−)	L3D
Receive from basis swap (+)	L3D − $0.25
Pay to basis swap (−)	Index
Receive from market (+)	Index

Profit on trade: $0.05 * 30 contracts = $15,000

FJS has completely hedged both the fixed-price risk and the basis risk. Regardless of where futures prices or Permian prices go, the end-result of the trade will be a $0.05 per MMBtu profit (or $15,000) for FJS. A fixed-float futures swap can always be used in place of trading actual futures contracts. This particular example, and any other trade where the L3D price is a component of the trade, demonstrates how the use of a futures swap could be a more efficient hedge in that it eliminates liquidation risk at expiration. The following table confirms the outcome of this trade as it shows various price assumptions for April Permian index and L3D April.

Index	FJS rec.'s L3D	Futures from Mkt.	Futures Bought	Pay to Sold	Rec. from Basis Swap	Pay to Basis Swap	Total Supplier	Net Profit/(Loss)
A $2.05	$1.45	$1.75	$1.45	$2.05	$2.05	$1.20	$1.75	$15,000
B $1.75	$1.75	$1.75	$1.75	$2.05	$1.75	$1.50	$1.75	$15,000
C $1.45	$2.05	$1.45	$2.05	$2.05	$1.45	$1.80	$1.75	$15,000

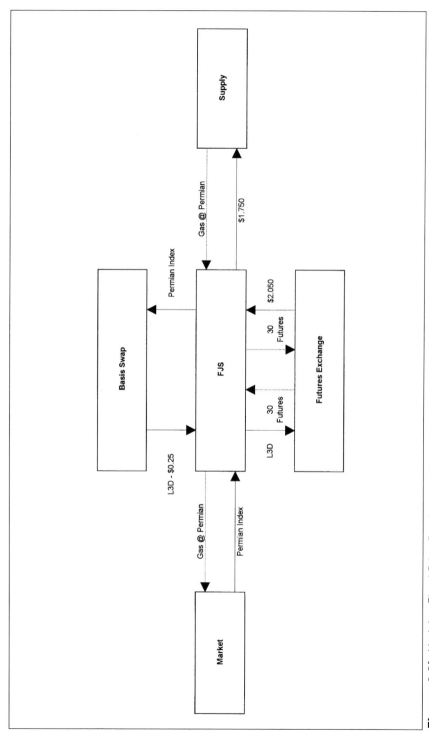

Figure 4.9b Hedging Fixed-Price Purchase at Alternate Delivery Location with Futures

Factors That Affect Basis Differentials

This segment is intended to provide novice basis swap traders with a better understanding of how the value of basis swaps changes.

Basis, in the natural gas market, is the difference in value between gas at one delivery point and gas at another. The actual basis differential of a particular location to another location is affected by changes in the value of gas at that particular location relative to the change in value of gas at the other location (a futures contract delivery point).

In trading natural gas basis swaps, the following events can cause the basis swap differential of a particular location (index) for a contract month to change:

a   futures price changes, no change in alternate location prices
b   fixed price for physical gas at the location changes, no change on futures price, or
c   a combination of a) and b) as long as the changes do not correlate (i.e., futures price increases $0.10 and fix price for physical decreases $0.10 or vice versa).

Therefore, to understand, and hopefully anticipate, the fluctuations in the basis differential of gas at an alternate location, a basis trader must be aware of both the supply and demand fundamentals of the physical market at that location, as well as the supply and demand fundamentals of the physical market at the futures contract delivery point, and how changes in these fundamentals will affect prices at each location. The basis trader, therefore, is essentially trading two markets (or more if trading more than one basis location) at the same time. In addition, because basis swaps reference an L3D price for the corresponding futures contract month at that futures contract delivery point, the trader must have an understanding of the factors changing the price of that futures contract (e.g., technically trading market, local-driven market). It is not an easy job.

The most important factor affecting the price of natural gas at a particular location is the current and anticipated weather pattern at that location. Different weather patterns at different locations, therefore, can affect prices in one location relative to another.

For example, let's suppose a basis swap trader has an opportunity to sell a Permian basis swap to a customer at L3D minus $0.30. Furthermore, let's assume the trader expects demand to increase in the Northeastern United States consuming region in the coming weeks due to colder weather, thereby causing the nearby futures contract price to rise in anticipation of rising fixed-price physical supply at Henry Hub (the location where most supply for this region's demand is purchased). What effect will this rise in futures prices have on the market differential for Permian basis swaps? The answer depends on what effect the colder-than-normal temperatures in the region will have on prices in West Texas (Permian Basin). Let's assume the trader anticipates futures prices will rise $0.10 at Henry due to the expected change in the weather pattern. The trader can make the following assumptions about resulting prices in the Permian and their likelihood of occurrence based on experience:

Permian Price Change	Likelihood of Occurrence
1. fall more than $0.10	5%
2. fall between $0.01 to $0.10	10%
3. remain unchanged	60%
4. rise between $0.01 to $0.10	20%
5. rise more than $0.10	5%

From the information (trader's forecast) in the table above, it appears that if futures prices rise by $0.10, there is only a 5% chance that Permian prices will rise by more than $0.10 as a result. In other words, given the current market basis differential for Permian of L3D minus $0.30, the trader expects only a 5% chance that the differential will tighten due to Permian fixed prices rising at a faster rate than Henry Hub fixed prices. In fact, the trader forecasts a 60% chance that Permian prices will remain unchanged even if Henry Hub prices rise. If this were the case, the trader would expect the market basis differential for Permian basis swaps to widen to L3D minus $0.40. Therefore, by selling the Permian basis swap to her customer at L3D minus $0.30, and paying L3D minus $0.40 to buy it back after futures prices rise, the trader anticipates making a $0.10 profit on the trade.

Index Swaps

Financial swaps used in the natural gas market have algebraic properties and identities (similar to mathematical equations) which allow them to be manipulated to produce other types of natural gas swaps or simplify physical natural gas pricing structures. The fixed-float index swap is one such product which fits this category.

A fixed-float index swap is the combination of two *other* natural gas swaps—a fixed-float futures swap, and a basis swap. In algebraic format:

Fixed-Float Index Swap = Fixed-Float Futures Swap + Basis Swap

That is, the desired effect of buying a fixed-float futures swap and buying a basis swap for a particular location can be achieved by simply buying a fixed-float index swap for that particular location. Likewise, by selling a fixed-float futures swap and selling a basis swap, the same desired outcome can be achieved by simply selling a fixed-float index swap.

Mechanics of Fixed-Float Index Swaps

Fixed-float index swaps (hereafter referred to as index swaps) are the simplest natural gas swaps in use today. The buyer of an Index swap pays a fixed price to the seller, and receives an index price from the seller in return. The seller, therefore, receives the fixed price from the buyer, and pays the index price to the buyer in return (Fig. 4.10).

Figure 4.10 Generic Index Swap

The fixed price in an index swap is a negotiated number, and the Index price references an agreed upon location. (An index swap, due to the nature of its component parts, is used exclusively for hedging or trading natural gas at locations other than the futures contract delivery point.) The index component of the swap is easily understood. When hedging a physical trade, or speculating at a given location, use the appropriate index for that location. The negotiated fixed price is slightly more complicated.

The Fixed-Price Component of Index Swaps

Aside from asking an OTC trader or an OTC broker for the fixed-price market for an index swap, how can this fixed price be determined? The fixed price component, or leg, of an index swap is derived from the fixed-price leg of a futures swap and the basis differential leg of a basis swap. That is, the fixed-price component of an index swap is simply the fixed price of a futures swap, adjusted by the basis differential for that particular index. So, if futures (and theoretically futures swaps) are trading $2.00, and the Permian basis swaps for the same month are currently trading L3D minus $0.25, the fixed-price component of a Permian index swap is worth $1.75. It's that simple.

Let's compare the end-result of a transaction where FJS trading company pays $1.90 for a fixed-float Permian index swap, and one where FJS pays both $2.30 for a fixed-float futures swap, and L3D minus $0.40 for a Permian basis swap. (For each example, assume Permian index equals $1.95) Figure 4.11 illustrates the index swap transaction and a schedule of payments and receipts for FJS follows.

Receive from Index swap (+) $1.95
Pay to Index swap (−) $1.90

Profit / loss on trade + $0.05 per contract x number of contracts

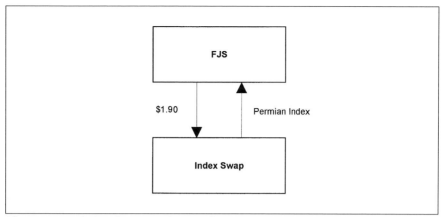

Figure 4.11 Index Swap vs. Futures Swap with Basis Swap - Buy Index Swap

Figure 4.12 illustrates the combined futures swap and basis swap transactions and is a schedule of payments and receipts for FJS.

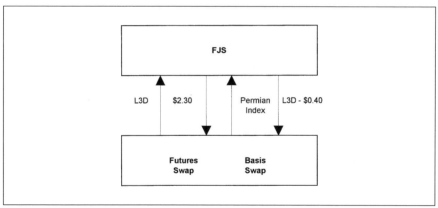

Fig. 4.12 Index Swap vs. Futures Swap with Basis Swap - Sell Basis Swap and buy Futures Swap

Pay to futures swap (−)	$2.30
Receive from futures swap (+)	L3D
Pay to basis swap (−)	L3D − $0.40
Receive from Index swap (+)	$1.95
Profit / loss on trade	+$0.05 per contract x number of contracts

As you can see, FJS could have substituted the index swap with both a basis swap and a futures swap, and would have achieved the same end-result. In fact, FJS could have done the basis swap and the futures swap with two different counterparties!

Although buying or selling a basis swap and a futures swap might seem more complicated and tedious than simply buying or selling an index swap, the profit or loss on a trade can often be improved through a better ultimate fixed price for the index swap by obtaining better prices in the basis swap and the futures swap. In the above example, for instance, if FJS were able to pay $2.30 (same price) for the futures swap from one party, but could pay L3D minus $0.42 for the basis swap from a different party, FJS could make an additional $0.02 per contract on the trade. Fixed-float index swap arbitrageurs make money by buying or selling the basis swap and the futures swap separately, and then selling or buying them together as a fixed-float Index swap package at a higher or lower price, respectively

As an alternative to using futures swaps, futures contracts can be substituted, although this requires an unwind previous to the last three trading days, or successful liquidation of the contracts at the L3D price.

Example of Selling a Fixed-Float Index Swap

To illustrate an example of selling a fixed-float Index swap, let's assume that FJS trading company has paid $2.00 to a natural gas producer for gas at Transco Zone 3 for September (Sep.) during bid week (last week in August), and has sold this supply to a market at the Sep. Transco Zone 3 index (Fig. 4.13).

At this point, we are only concerned with the financial component of this transaction (i.e. the fixed price paid, and the index price received). We will assume that the physical volume bought (10,000 MMBtu/d) is equal to the physical volume sold (10,000 MMBtu/d) and that the total volumes at the end of the month are equal to 300,000. Because index is not published until the first day of Sep., FJS has bought fixed and sold floating, and is exposed to any discrepancy between the two prices on the payment date. For simplicity, let's examine only three possible outcomes of this trade depending on where Sep. Transco Zone 3 index actually is: $2.05, $2.00, and $1.95.

Based on these index assumptions, FJS will make a total profit of $15,000, break even, or lose $15,000. It sounds like FJS is rolling the dice at a craps table. In a sense, this type of a trade is a gamble on where index comes out, but a savvy trading company like FJS may have a strong enough conviction about the market going up and, as such, may feel the position is worth the risk. If this is the case, there is no need for a swap, but for this example, where the direction of the market is not so clear, FJS decides to enter into a fixed-float Transco Zone 3 index swap with XYZ swap trading company.

Since FJS is selling gas at index to the market, it will receive this payment. Also, because FJS is paying a fixed price of $2.00 to the producer for the gas, it will need this payment. So, FJS is looking for a Transco Zone 3 swap *counterparty* needing to receive an index payment and willing to pay a fixed price for that payment. FJS is therefore a seller of the fixed-float index swap. Let's assume that XYZ is in need of index, for an opposite transaction, and will pay $2.02 for it. FJS and XYZ enter into a swap wherein XYZ will pay $2.02 to

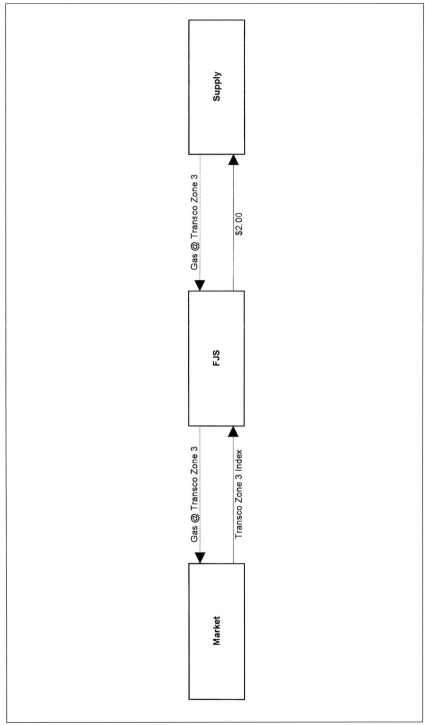

Figure 4.13 Selling a Fixed-Float Index Swap to Convert Index Sale to a Fixed Price—Fixed Floating Risk

FJS, and FJS will pay Index to XYZ on the first of Sep. when index becomes known. In addition, both parties agree to do the swap for 10,000 MMBtu/d for a total volume of 300,000 MMBtu. Remember, a fixed-float swap of any kind is only a financial transaction and, although it is based on a specified volume in order to calculate payments, no *additional* physical product is transferred between the two parties. Also, note that when index is equal to the fixed price, the two would-be payments by each party cancel out, therefore eliminating the need to exchange payments altogether. Figure 4.14 illustrates how this financial transaction would be added to the physical transaction.

By separating the two transactions, let's see what the "net" result to FJS trading company would be for each of the above index assumptions.

Index Assumption	FJS pays Producer	FJS receives from Market	Swap Payment	Swap Receipt	Total Net Profit/Loss
1. $2.05	$2.00	$2.05	$2.05	$2.02	$0.02 x 300,000
2. $2.00	$2.00	$2.00	$2.00	$2.02	$0.02 x 300,000
3. $1.95	$2.00	$1.95	$1.95	$2.02	$0.02 x 300,000

Regardless of the index value, FJS has passed through the floating price (index) in return for a known fixed price, in this case $2.02, netting a locked-in $6,000 profit on the trade. The profit is more easily calculated as simply the difference between the fixed price FJS is paying the producer for the gas, and the fixed price FJS receives from selling the fixed-float index swap to XYZ, multiplied by the volume of gas traded. Although FJS will forgo any profit if Index is greater than $2.02, it has completely eliminated the risk of making anything less than a $0.02 / MMBtu margin. This is clearly easier than doing a fixed-float futures swap and a Transco Zone 3 basis swap!

Example of Buying a Fixed-Float Index Swap

If the tables were turned in the above example with FJS buying gas at index and selling it at $2.00, the mechanics of the transaction would be reversed. Since FJS would be selling gas to the market at a fixed price, it will receive this known payment. Also, because FJS is paying an index price to the producer, it will need this payment. So, FJS is looking for a Transco Zone 3 index swap counterparty needing to receive a fixed-price payment and willing to pay the unknown index price for that payment. Let's assume that XYZ needs a fixed price of $1.98 for an opposite transaction and will pay index to FJS for it. FJS trading company and XYZ enter into a swap wherein XYZ will pay index to FJS, and FJS will pay $1.98 to XYZ on the first of Sep. when index becomes known. Figure 4.15 illustrates how this transaction would look on paper.

By separating the two transactions again, let's see what the net result to FJS trading company would be for each of the same Transco Zone 3 index assumptions from the first example.

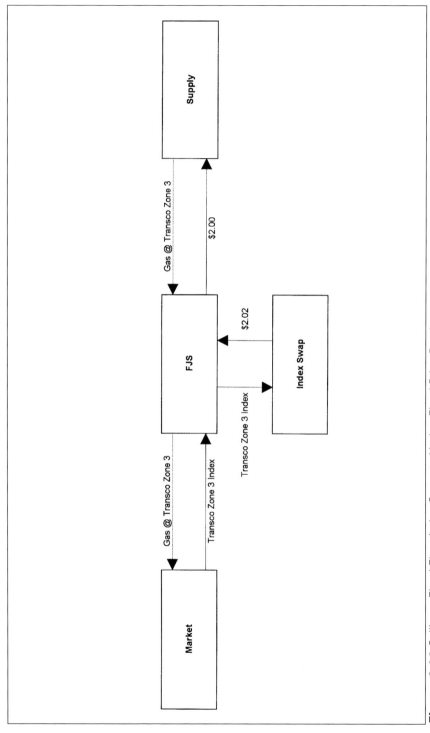

Figure 4.14 Selling a Fixed-Float Index Swap to Hedge Fixed-Price Purchase

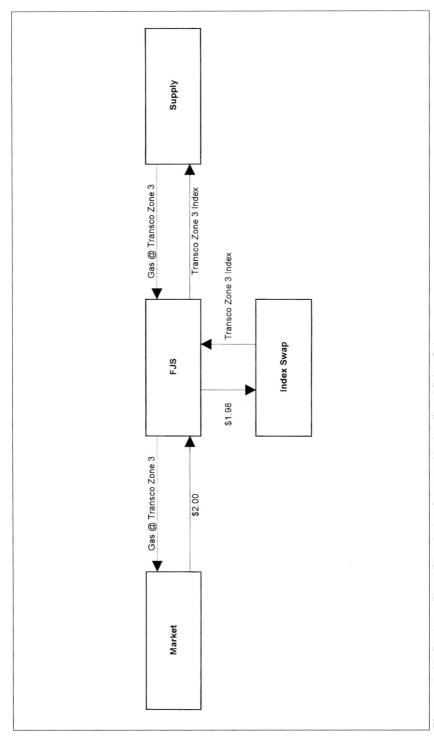

Figure 4.15 Buying a Fixed-Float Index Swap to Hedge Fixed-Price Sale

Index	FJS pays Assumption	FJS receives Producer	Swap from Market	Swap Payment Receipt	Total Net Profit/Loss
1. $2.05	$2.05	$2.00	$1.985	$2.05	$0.02 x 300,000
2. $2.00	$2.00	$2.00	$1.98	$2.00	$0.02 x 300,000
3. $1.95	$1.95	$2.00	$1.98	$1.95	$0.02 x 300,000

Regardless of the index value, FJS has passed through the known fixed price in exchange for an unknown floating price (index), which is what payment to the producer is based on. Again, this hedge has locked-in a $6,000 profit on the trade. The profit can again be more easily calculated as the difference between the fixed price FJS is receiving from the market for selling the gas and the fixed price FJS pays to XYZ when it buys the fixed-float index swap, multiplied by the volume of gas traded. Although FJS will forgo any profit if index is lower than $1.95, it has completely eliminated the risk of making anything less than a $0.02 / MMBtu margin.

Making a Market Using Fixed-Float Index Swaps

Fixed-float index swaps should be used by any trading company that wants to enhance its customer service by being able to offer either a fixed price or an Index price at any time to its producer and end user customers. Before the fixed-float index swap market existed, if a trader thought prices were about to fall, he or she would not quote a producer a fixed price or would quote one that was embarrassingly low relative to the current price level. The trader might retreat even further by quoting only an index price for safety. But, as the producer probably shared the same market opinion and therefore wanted to sell at a fixed price somewhere near the current market, the producer would probably look elsewhere for someone who was willing to buy gas in that manner. Now, however, if a trader actively participates in the fixed-float index swap market, he or she should be able to quote a reasonable fixed price for either a producer or end user customer, regardless of his or her own opinion of the future direction of the market. As a result, through the use of these swaps, savvy trading companies are able to *make a market*—quote a buy price and simultaneously quote a sell price—at any time for fixed-price gas at any location where an Index price is published, for any month or months in the future.

Accounting for Change in Value of Index

In the case of buying or selling gas at a fixed price and thereafter selling or buying a fixed-float index swap to eliminate the fixed-price exposure, how is the best way to value the gas in terms of index once the transaction has been hedged? The answer depends on whether physical gas is being bought at a fixed price or sold at a fixed price, and at what fixed price the hedge is done.

When buying gas at a fixed price and selling a fixed-float index swap to hedge, simply add the difference between the fixed price paid for the gas versus the fixed price received from the index swap to index if it is a negative difference, or subtract the difference between the fixed price paid for the gas versus the fixed price received from the Index swap from index if it is a positive difference.

For example, if you pay $2.00 for gas and sell an index swap at $2.05, you are long gas at index minus $0.05. If you pay $2.00 for gas and sell an index swap at $2.00, you are long gas at index. And, if you pay $2.00 for gas, sell index swap at $1.95, you are long gas at index + $0.05.

When selling gas at a fixed price and buying a fixed-float index swap to hedge, simply subtract the difference between the fixed price received for the gas versus the fixed price paid to the index swap from index if it is a negative difference, or add the difference between the fixed price received for the gas versus the fixed price paid to the index swap to index if it is a positive difference.

For example, if you sell gas at $2.00 and pay $1.95 for an index swap, you are short gas at index plus $0.05. If you sell gas at $2.00 and pay $2.00 for an index swap, you are short gas at index. And if you sell gas at $2.00 and pay $2.05 for an index swap, you are short gas at index minus $0.05.

Trading Application of Fixed-Float Index Swaps

Let's suppose a trading company just bought an extremely large volume of gas in the Permian Basin at index flat from a producer under a long-term contract. The trading director for that region decides it would be in the best interest of the company if it sold some of the supply before the next bid week cycle. Consequently, the trading director asks all traders to sell Permian gas at index plus $.01 or better (higher) for the following month.

Toni, a trader at the company, decides to make as many phone calls as she can to the buyers she knows to try to sell Permian gas at index plus $0.01. At the end of a long day she hasn't sold a single MMBtu because the buyers were only willing to pay index flat or fixed prices. She needs another approach.

The next day, Toni has an opportunity to sell 10,000 MMBtu/d at $1.75 to a buyer in the Permian for the next month. Because she is supposed to sell at index plus $0.01 or higher, Toni realizes that she will need to do a fixed-float index swap if she sells gas at a fixed price to convert the fixed price into an Index price. To determine whether this is a good fixed-price for Permian, and since she doesn't want to take fixed-price risk, Toni calls an OTC broker to obtain the market for a Permian fixed-float index swap. When she calls the broker, he responds, "Permian fixed-float is $1.71 bid at $1.73 for next month." Since she needs to pay a fixed price for the swap and in return receive index, Toni is really only interested in the offer. She calculates that this sale not only meets the sales price target of index plus $0.01, but is actually worth index plus $0.02, or $3,100 more! Below is a quick schedule of payments and receipts for this example.

Receive from market (+)	$1.75
Pay to swap (−)	$1.73
Receive from swap (+)	Index
Effective sales price index plus	$0.02

What Toni has done is net the difference between the two fixed prices, even though one is for physical gas and the other is for a swap, and because it is a positive difference she has applied that gain to the index sales price. As a result, since the effective sales price would meet and even exceed the goal set by her trading director, Toni buys the fixed-float Permian index swap for $1.73 and simultaneously sells the physical gas in the Permian at $1.75 to her customer. The fixed-float index swap was just the tool Toni needed to reach her goal of selling gas above index plus $0.01 without taking fixed-price risk.

It should now be obvious how important fixed-float index swaps are as a trading tool. Although the most common use of this type of swap is for situations encountered by traders, such as in the example above, there are other popular ways in which they are used by other market participants in managing risk.

Index Swap Applications for Producers and End Users

Most producers will often sell a large percentage of a their total available supply to various buyers under long-term, short-term, or even one month contracts which are based on an index price at the point where the supply is located. Similarly, end users enter into the same types of contracts with various sellers. This is a common practice for two reasons—to sell/buy supply at or close to the market price and to secure reliable market/supply for various durations. Therefore, if a producer has sold 90% of its supply under these types of contracts, and, during a particular bid week, has sold the remaining 10% at fixed prices but still thinks prices are going to fall further, it can sell fixed-float index swaps in order to make a profit from the swaps if the index falls to a lower level than the fixed price they receive from the swap buyers. The result is an increase in the producer's effective sales price to its physical sales customers, priced at index, by that amount. In the case of an end user, with a secured portion of supply under index-based contracts, it can buy fixed-float index swaps to make a profit from the swaps if the index rises to a higher level than the fixed price. This profit can be applied to the index price it must pay to the suppliers, thus reducing its effective purchase price by that amount. Of course, if the market should go the opposite direction for either the producer or end user after they have done fixed-float index swaps, their effective prices would be reduced or increased, respectively.

Example of End User Application. The following example will help illustrate how an end user can fix the price of index-priced physical gas already in its portfolio. For an industrial end-user concerned with prices rising, buying fixed-float Index swaps is a means of locking in a fixed buy price for its index-priced supply. If the end user has supply in its portfolio at an average price of

index flat, and buys a fixed-float index swap at $1.95, its effective buy price will be $1.95.

Pay to swap (−)	$1.95
Receive from swap (+)	Index
Pay to supplier (−)	Index
Effective buy price	$1.95

Example of Producer Application. For a producer concerned with falling prices, selling fixed-float index swaps is a means of locking in a fixed sales price for its index-priced supply. If a producer has sales in its portfolio at an average price of index plus $0.02, for example, and sells a fixed-float index swap at $1.95, its effective sales price will equate to $1.97.

Receive from swap (+)	$1.95
Pay to swap (-)	Index
Receive from market (+)	Index + $0.02
Effective sales price	$1.97

Index Swap Applications for Speculators

Fixed-float index swaps are also used for speculating by trading companies, such as hedge funds or banks, that are not in the business of trading physical natural gas. Fixed-float index swaps provide an investment vehicle other than futures contracts for trading and profiting from their market views at these alternate locations. In addition, an index swap can be converted into either a futures swap, or a basis swap, by stripping out the unwanted component. A fixed-float index swap is the combination of two other natural gas swaps—a fixed-float futures swap and a basis swap. Or, in algebraic format:

Fixed-Float Index Swap = Fixed-Float Futures Swap + Basis Swap

Therefore, if we were to strip out the fixed-float futures swap, we would be left with a basis swap. Similarly, if we were to strip out the basis swap, we would be left with a fixed-float futures swap. For example, if a speculator sold a Permian Index swap at $1.75, and subsequently paid L3D minus $0.25 for a Permian basis swap, he would essentially be short a futures swap at $2.00. Figure 4.16 illustrates these steps.

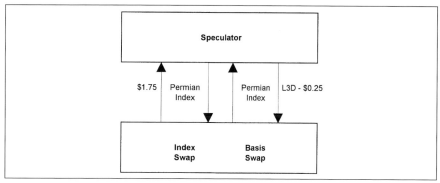

Figure 4.16 Creating Short Futures Swap Position by Selling Index Swap and Buying Basis Swap

Receive from Index swap (+)	$1.75
Pay to Index swap (−)	Index
Receive from Basis swap (+)	Index
Pay to Basis swap (−)	L3D − $0.25
Effective position	Receive $1.75
	Pay L3D − $0.25
or equivalently,	Receive $2.00
	Pay L3D

Therefore, from the definition of a fixed-float futures swap, the speculator would be effectively short a futures swap at $2.00.

The next example illustrates the effective position resulting from stripping out the fixed-float futures swap from an index swap.

If a speculator sold a Permian index swap at $1.75, and subsequently paid $2.00 for a fixed-float futures swap, he would essentially be short a Permian basis swap at L3D minus $0.25. Figure 4.17 illustrates these steps.

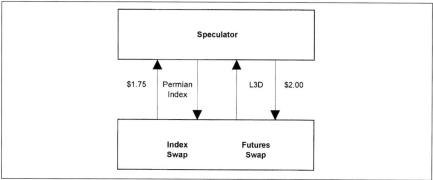

Figure 4.17 Creating Short Basis Swap Position by Selling Index Swap and Buying Futures Swap

Pay to Index swap (−)   Index
Receive from Index swap (+) $1.75
Pay to futures swap (−) $2.00
Receive from futures swap (+) L3D

Effective position   Pay Index
                              Pay $0.25
                              Receive L3D

or equivalently,   Pay Index
                              Receive L3D − $0.25

Therefore, from the definition of a basis swap, the speculator would be effectively short a Permian basis swap at L3D minus $0.25 (i.e., receives L3D plus or minus differential, pays index). The following diagram indicates how a short index swap position is created by selling a futures swap and selling a basis swap.

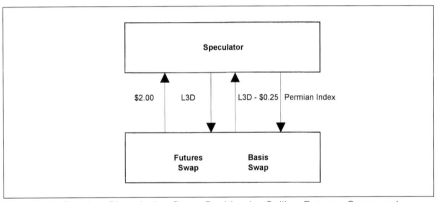

Fig. 4.18 Creating Short Index Swap Position by Selling Futures Swap and Selling Basis Swap

Manipulating fixed-float index swaps in these ways is not done exclusively for the purpose of speculating. In fact, many traders keep track of all three markets and continuously analyze the various prices of combinations to enhance profit margins on their trades. For example, if a trader has sold a futures swap to a customer at $2.00, and can either pay $2.00 for a futures swap, or pay $1.75 for a Permian index swap and sell a Permian basis swap at L3D minus $0.24 (resulting in a long futures swap at $1.99), the trader would probably take the extra time and make the extra effort by doing the index swap and the basis swap trades in order to double the profit on the futures swap sale to the customer.

Also, keep in mind that index swaps, basis swaps, and futures swaps can be traded in any order to achieve a position in a different swap.

For example, if you sell a futures swap at $2.00, sell a basis swap at L3D minus $0.25 you have a short index swap at $1.75, but if you pay $2.00 for a futures swap and pay L3D minus $0.25 for a basis swap, you have a long index swap at $1.75.

The reader should be aware, however, that if the direction of the two components in the above examples are not the same, the resulting position is effectively two different positions, the profitability of which would depend on the profit or loss of both positions combined. Let's examine the potential impact from doing one such trade. This trade is extremely risky and should only be traded, if ever, as long as the degree of risk is fully understood by the trader and company management.

What are the profit and loss parameters in the case where a trader has sold a futures swap at $2.00, and paid L3D minus $0.25 for a Permian basis swap? Figure 4.19 and the schedule of payments and receipts following show how the cash flows are mismatched.

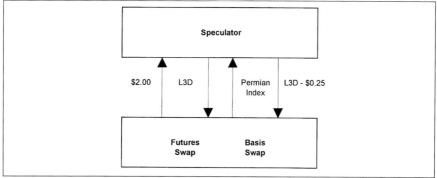

Figure 4.19 Combining Futures Swap Sale and Basis Swap Purchase Yields Two Positions

Receive from futures swap (+)	$2.00
Pay to futures swap (−)	L3D
Receive from basis swap (+)	Index
Pay to basis swap (−)	L3D − $0.25

Break-even where:	$2.00 − L3D + Index − (L3D − $0.25) = 0
or equivalently where:	$2.00 − L3D + Index = L3D − $0.25
or equivalently where:	$2.00 + Index = 2xL3D − $0.25
or equivalently where:	Index = 2xL3D − $2.25

The table below illustrates the outcomes given various assumptions for Index and L3D:

Index	L3D	Rec. from fut. swap	Pay to fut. swap	Rec. from Basis Swap	Pay to Basis Swap	Net Profit/(Loss)
1. $1.75	$2.00	$2.00	$2.00	$1.75	$1.75	$0.00
2. $1.85	$2.00	$2.00	$2.00	$1.85	$1.75	$0.10
3. $1.65	$2.00	$2.00	$2.00	$1.65	$1.75	($0.10)
4. $1.85	$2.10	$2.00	$2.10	$1.85	$1.85	($0.10)
5. $1.65	$1.90	$2.00	$1.90	$1.65	$1.65	$0.10
6. $1.95	$2.10	$2.00	$2.10	$1.95	$1.85	$0.00
7. $1.75	$2.10	$2.00	$2.10	$1.75	$1.85	($0.20)
8. $1.75	$1.90	$2.00	$1.90	$1.75	$1.65	$0.20

To summarize, if the trader has sold a futures swap at $2.00 and paid L3D minus $0.25 for a Permian basis swap, the trade will be break even if both the actual basis differential of Permian is equal to L3D minus $0.25, and the L3D price is equal to $2.00. The trade will make money if the actual Permian basis differential is tighter than L3D minus $0.25, and the L3D price is less than or equal to $2.00. If both the actual Permian basis differential is not equal to L3D minus $0.25, and the L3D price is not equal to $2.00 and if one of the profitable scenario does not occur, above is not true, the trade will lose money. However, if the actual Permian basis differential is tighter than L3D minus $0.25, and the L3D price is less than $2.00, the trade would be more profitable than had only the basis swap or the futures swap been bought or sold, respectively. It should now be clear to the reader that to say this trade is extremely risky would be an understatement.

Swing Swaps

In the physical market, a *swing* transaction is a purchase or sale under an interruptible contract which is renegotiated (in terms of price and volume) day-by-day. These types of transactions are extremely popular and make up the bulk of the trading activity in the day-to-day natural gas market. However, there are times during the month when market participants have opportunities to enter into baseload or firm transactions for the remaining days of that month. Price discovery for such odd tenures used to be difficult if not impossible in extreme cases. For example, suppose that on the fifth day of the month a buyer calls a trader and wants to buy gas from the 18th through the 27th of the current month. If prices on the fifth day are trading $2.00, what price should the trader offer to the buyer for gas from the 18th through the 27th? The price either came out of thin air or from someone who had supply available for that exact tenure that the trader could buy first and then resell to his buyer at a higher price. This process was sloppy, complicated,sometimes, very risky. The advent of swing swaps brought a new hedging and trading instrument to the natural gas market which has helped market participants with price discovery, hedging, and speculating in the day-to-day cash market.

Definition of a Swing Swap

A *swing swap* is a fixed-float index swap that references the average of daily indexes published by **Gas Daily** as a floating price instead of the commonly referenced monthly indexes published by **Inside FERC Gas Market Report**. Gas Daily *publishes a high and low daily price range for the same locations for* which IFGMR publishes monthly indexes. The daily index is calculated as the simple average of the high and low prices of the published range for that location on that trading day. If the swap is longer than one day in tenure, the simple average of each of the daily indexes is used as the floating price.) The buyer of a swing swap typically pays a fixed price and receives the daily index, or the average of the daily indexes for the tenure of the swap. A sample of how to calculate the floating price in a hypothetical 5-day swing swap follows.

Date	High Price	Low Price	Index = (High + Low) / 2
5/10/95	$2.10	$2.05	$2.075
5/11/95	$2.07	$2.01	$2.04
5/12/95	$2.00	$1.98	$1.99
5/13/95	$2.05	$2.02	$2.035
5/14/95	$2.18	$2.04	$2.11
		Average =	$2.05

The standard calculation for weekends and holidays is to use the same daily price for Monday, or the first day after the holiday, as plugged in prices for Saturday and Sunday, or the holiday.)

If a trader had paid more than $2.04 for this swing swap, it would have resulted in a loss, and vice versa had the trader paid less.

Applications for Swing Swaps

Swing swaps are used to hedge fixed-price risk in day-to-day physical transactions, discover price information, and also to speculate on changes in prices in the day-to-day market. In other words, a swing swap is essentially a futures swap which derives its value from fixed prices in the physical market during a given month instead of a futures contract for a given month. Below is an example of how swing swaps can be used by producers to take advantage of rising fixed prices for physical gas during a current month.

Example of Producer Application

Let's suppose FJS production company has sold all of its physical gas supply for the month of Jan. at $2.00 to an end user in the Permian basin under a firm contract. Since FJS has sold the gas to the end user under a firm contract, the end user is obligated to take all of the supply every day for the entire month of Jan. and pay $2.00 for it regardless of price changes during the month. On the eighth day of January, the weather patterns change such that FJS believes prices in the Permian will rise due to increasing demand from colder weather in the Western United States. Although the producer has already sold its supply at one fixed price for the entire month, it can still participate in the price action during the month with a swing swap. To take advantage of the expected increase in prices for the remainder of the month, FJS pays $2.00 to XYZ for a Permian swing swap for the 10th of Jan through the 31st (assume prices were unchanged from first of the month levels over the first nine days). Figure 4.20 illustrates what this transaction would look like after FJS buys the swing swap from XYZ.

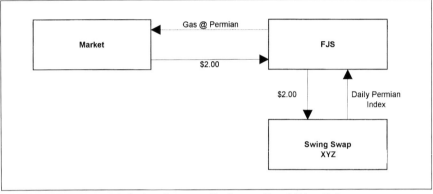

Figure 4.20 Buying A Swing Swap to Re-float a Fixed-Price Sale

The schedule of payments and receipts below shows the new effective price FJS will realize during the remainder of the month.

Receive from end user (+) $2.00
Pay to swing swap (-) $2.00
Receive from swing swap (+) average (daily Permian index 1/10 – 1/31)

Effective sales price   average (daily Permian index 1/10 – 1/31)

It should be fairly obvious that FJS has passed through the fixed price it is receiving from the end user in exchange for a floating price which will reflect changes in fixed prices for the remainder of the month. Therefore, if daily fixed prices in the Permian for the remainder of the month average higher than $2.00, FJS will increase its effective sale price. On the other hand, if daily fixed prices in the Permian for the remainder of the month average lower than $2.00, FJS will reduce its effective sale price.

Example of End User Application

Let's suppose XYZ end user has paid $2.00 to a producer for all of its physical gas supply for the month of January in the Permian basin under a firm contract. Since XYZ bought the gas from the producer under a firm contract, the producer is obligated to make the supply available to XYZ every day for the entire month and in return, receive $2.00 for it regardless of price changes during the month. On the eighth day of January, the weather patterns change such that XYZ believes prices in the Permian will fall due to reduced demand from balmy weather in the Western United States. Although the end user has already paid one fixed price for its supply for the entire month, it can still participate in the price action during the month with a swing swap. To take advantage of the expected decrease in prices for the remainder of the month, XYZ sells a Permian swing swap for the 10th of Jan through the 31st (assume prices were unchanged from first of the month levels over the first nine days of January) at $2.00 to FJS trading company. Figure 4.21 illustrates what this transaction would look like after XYZ sells the swing swap to FJS.

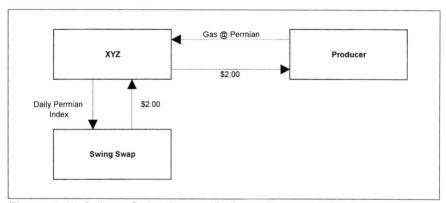

Figure 4.21 Selling a Swing Swap to Re-float a Fixed-Price Purchase

This schedule of payments and receipts shows the new effective price XYZ will realize for the remainder of the month.

Pay to Permian supplier (−) $2.00
Receive from swing swap (+) $2.00
Pay to swing swap (−)   Average (daily Permian index 1/10 − 1/31)

Effective purchase price   Average (daily Permian index 1/10 − 1/31)

XYZ has passed through the fixed price it is paying to the Permian supplier in exchange for a floating price which will reflect changes in fixed prices for the remainder of the month. Therefore, if daily fixed prices in the Permian for the remainder of the month average lower than $2.00, XYZ will reduce its

effective purchase price. On the other hand, if daily fixed prices in the Permian for the remainder of the month average higher than $2.00, XYZ will increase its effective purchase price.

Hedging a Swing Swap Purchase or Sale

If a trader has an opportunity to buy or sell a swing swap, but doesn't have an opportunity to offset that trade with another swing swap, how can a trader hedge it against adverse price movement in the day-to-day physical market? To hedge a swing swap, a trader must have the capability of trading physical gas in the day-to-day market at the specific location referenced in the swing swap.

For example, let's suppose a trader has an opportunity to sell a January Permian swing swap to a customer at $2.00. Furthermore, let's assume the trader can pay $1.95 for baseload Permian supply for the month. Remember, a baseload transaction is one in which neither party is legally obligated to perform, although each agrees to the terms and conditions on a best-efforts basis. Baseload contracts should be used when hedging swing swaps instead of swing or firm contracts. Figure 4.22 illustrates the trader's position at this point.

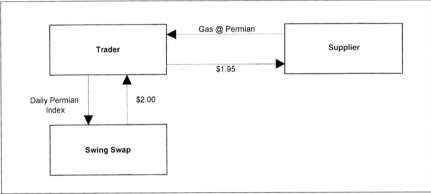

Figure 4.22 Hedging Swing Swap Sale by Buying Fixed-Price Physical Gas

The trader has effectively passed through the fixed price, and has earned a $0.05 / MMBtu margin thus far, in exchange for the daily Permian index for January. However, the trader is still long the physical supply since the Permian swing swap is only a financial transaction. To complete the trade, therefore, the trader must successfully sell the baseload supply in the day-to-day market at the middle or higher end of the daily price range published for the Permian each day during the month of January. This would effectively give the trader the daily index which could then be passed along to the swing swap. Figure 4.23 and the schedule of payments and receipts which follows show the completed transaction and the resulting profit on the trade, assuming the trader is successful in selling the gas at exactly the average of all daily Permian indexes in January.

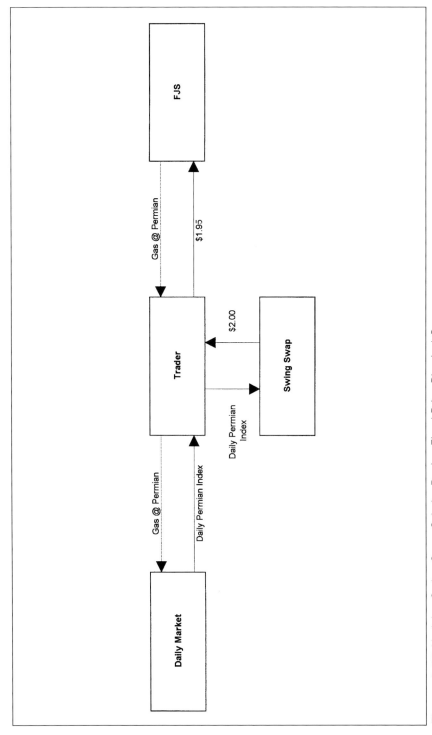

Figure 4.23 Hedging Swing Swap Sale by Buying Fixed-Price Physical Gas

Pay to Permian supplier (-)	$1.95
Receive from swing swap (+)	$2.00
Pay to swing swap (−)	Average (daily Permian index 1/1 − 1/31)
Receive from day-to-day market (+)	Average (daily Permian index 1/1 − 1/31)
Net profit / (loss)	$0.05

Similarly, a trader can pay a fixed price for a swing swap to a customer if he or she can sell baseload gas for the entire month at a higher fixed price, and consequently buy gas in the day-to-day market each day during the month to cover the sale. The trader must be able to pay the daily index or lower each day in order to keep any margin which was built-in at the onset of the transaction. Additional profit can be made if the trader can effectively pay a lower price during the month than the daily index.

As mentioned previously, it is recommended that a baseload contract be used for the other side of a swing swap transaction instead of a swing or firm contract. This is recommended because of the lack of certainty of performance by other parties in the day-to-day market. In other words, because the trader hedging a swing swap must buy or sell gas in the day-to-day market in order to pay or receive the daily index each day to offset that component of the swing swap, he or she will most likely be buying or selling that supply from or to a party that is unsure of the reliability of its supply or market. In addition, although a swing contract is most likely used when transacting in the day-to-day market, the trader hedging a swing swap needs the same fixed price all month. This is most effectively done under a baseload contract.

Example of Speculative Applications

Speculators use swing swaps to participate in the fixed-price action in the cash market without the administrative burden of actually trading the physical gas. The most common trade is to either buy or sell swing swaps outright anticipating prices to either rise or fall, respectively. However, another speculative opportunity exists where swing swaps can be traded profitably with slightly less risk than an outright fixed-price position. This opportunity is called *spread trading* for either convergence or divergence.

Spread trading is the practice of taking a position in one month and offsetting it with an equal but opposite position in the previous or following month. The expectation is that the two prices will converge or diverge. *Convergence* is the effect of the price for a particular month, or time period, rising or falling to the same level or close to the same as those for another time period as it approaches. *Divergence* is the effect of prices for a particular month, or other time period, rising or falling away from those of another time period, as those time periods approach each other. The differences between prices of two months are called *month spreads*. In the futures market, to take advantage of converging prices, a futures trader will sell short the higher-priced month and buy long the lower-priced month in the same amount. This is called *selling the spread* and will be profitable if the two prices converge from the prices where the month spread position was initiated. Similarly, to take advantage of a divergence in prices between two months, a futures trader will buy long the higher-priced month and sell short the same amount of the lower-priced month. This is called *buying the spread* and will be profitable if the two prices diverge from the prices where the spread position was initiated.

Henry Hub (NYMEX) or Waha Hub (KCBT) swing swaps can be used to trade the convergence between current month fixed prices for physical gas, and the nearby futures contract with the expectation that cash and futures prices will converge as the end of the month approaches. Traders rarely trade the divergence between swing swap prices and the price of the nearby futures contract because these prices tend to converge as traders make and take delivery of physical gas at the futures expiration. Trading convergence between these prices is executed by buying a swing swap at one of these locations, and simultaneously offsetting that position with an equal size, but short position in the nearby month futures contract.

Unlike month spreads in the futures market, however, trading the convergence between cash prices and futures requires more work than just putting on the positions and taking them off when prices have either converged or diverged or when the earlier month futures contract expires. Because the floating price in the swing swap is an average of the daily indexes, that position will erode by one day's volume as each day's price is established, and subsequently factored into the monthly average. Therefore, it is necessary to close out an equal amount of the futures position each day to manage the spread properly. The futures position can be liquidated in larger portions at various times, although the correlation to the cash market might not be accurately reflected. In addition, weekend pricing specifics for swing swaps can vary among counterparties, however this erosion still requires the liquidation of three times the daily volume in futures contracts on either Friday or Monday. Furthermore, because futures expire five (KCBT) or six (NYMEX) business days prior to the end of the month, all remaining futures contracts are assumed to be liquidated on expiration day, thereby exposing the swing swap position to changes in the fixed price in the cash market for the last five or six days of the month. These types of convergence opportunities usually present themselves at the beginning of a new month in the cash market when the expired futures contract has been replaced with a new month.

Another common use for swing swaps is to integrate them into more complex, structured transactions for customers that need flexibility in pricing or flexibility in making or taking delivery of physical gas during the month.

EFPs

Definition of EFP

An *exchange of futures for physical* (EFP) is a contractual arrangement between two parties, under which one party will give futures contracts to the other and receive physical gas from that party in return. When transacting an EFP, both parties must agree on the following specifics:

a.   Posted Price — The price at which the futures contracts are transferred from one account to the other.

b.   Differential — The difference in value, if any, between the futures contracts and the physical gas.

c.   Delivery point — The location where one party will deliver and the other will receive the physical gas.

d   Size — The daily volume of product bought/sold and, equivalently, the total number of futures contracts to be exchanged.

e.   Invoice Price — The price paid by the buyer to the seller for the physical gas, calculated as the posted price plus the differential.

The quality of gas in the transaction is required (and assumed) to be of the same quality as that specified in the futures contract specifications.

The volume of natural gas traded under EFPs each month averages roughly 90% of the total volume taken to delivery directly at Henry Hub or through ADP's (alternate delivery points). Even though they are negotiated in the OTC market but transacted on the exchange, EFPs are extremely popular due to the many risk management objectives that can be achieved depending on the way in which they are traded.

Mechanics of an EFP

An EFP is a transaction in which one party will give futures contracts to the other and receive physical gas from that party in return. More specifically, the buyer of an EFP does the following:

1.   pays the invoice price to the seller for the physical (the posted price plus a negotiated differential)

2.   receives physical gas at the agreed upon delivery point (a location other than a futures contract delivery point) from the seller, and

3.   transfers futures contracts (which are valued at the posted price) from its futures account into the seller's account.

Alternately, the seller of an EFP does the following:

1. receives the invoice price (the posted price plus a negotiated EFP differential) from the buyer,

2. delivers physical gas at the agreed upon delivery point (a location other than a futures contract delivery point) to the buyer, and

3. transfers futures contracts (which are valued at the posted price) from its futures account into the buyer's account.

EFP Differential. The two most important elements of an EFP are the differential and the delivery location. These are the only components which are negotiated, due to their importance in the objective of the EFP transaction for each party. Since EFPs are traded at locations other than a futures contract delivery point, there is inherent basis risk in any EFP. Therefore, the EFP differential is negotiated between the two traders much like basis differentials are in basis swaps. In general, an EFP differential for a particular location should be approximately the same as the basis swap differential for that location.

EFP Delivery Point. The importance of the delivery point should be fairly self-explanatory. If a trader negotiates a fair differential for delivery at one location, the trader shouldn't agree to take delivery or make delivery of that gas at a location where the differential negotiated is not a fair differential for that location. For example, negotiating and buying an EFP with a differential of minus $0.02 (fair value on Transco at Zone 3), but then agreeing to receive that gas in the Permian basin (fair value approximately plus $0.40) would not contribute positively to the end result of the trade. In general, because the value of the gas at an agreed upon delivery location is reflected in the EFP differential, delivery and receipt of the gas should correspond only to that referenced delivery location.

EFP Posted Price . The invoice price has no effect on the end-result of the trade. This is due to the relationship between the calculation of the invoice price (posted price plus EFP differential), and the valuation of the futures contracts when they are transferred from the buyer's account to the seller's (posted price). Remember that a positive number added to a negative number reduces that positive number. If two EFP traders agree on a posted price of $100.00 and a differential of minus $0.25, the buyer of the EFP will pay $99.75 for the physical gas (invoice price), but the buyer's futures account will show a transfer out (sale) of futures contracts at $100.00 to the EFP seller's account.

Components and Properties of an EFP

An EFP is made up of three components (not to be confused with specifications)— a *basis swap*, *physical index gas*, and *futures contracts* valued at L3D. In algebraic format in terms of position:

Long EFP = long (+) basis swap, long (+) gas at index, and short (–) futures at L3D

Short EFP = short (–) basis swap, short (-) gas at index, and long (+) futures at L3D

A trader buying an EFP is essentially buying a basis swap for a particular location, buying index gas at that same location, and selling futures contracts valued at L3D. Likewise, a trader selling an EFP is essentially selling a basis swap for a particular location, selling index gas at that same location, and buying futures contracts valued at L3D.

Applications for EFPs

A natural gas EFP can be used to hedge any physical transaction at a delivery location other than a futures contract delivery point. In other words, because of the futures contract component, EFP's link the futures market to alternate delivery points in the physical market. Therefore, if an end user, for example, bought futures contracts as a hedge against rising prices, but needs the physical supply in Chicago instead of Henry Hub, the user can buy a Chicago EFP, thereby giving up futures contracts in exchange for physical gas at a Chicago delivery point.

The most outstanding and intriguing feature of EFPs is the ability of both the buyer and the seller in an EFP transaction to realize a different effective price for the same physical gas. In other words, if a producer sells an EFP to an end user, the producer can actually realize a higher effective price for the gas and the end user can actually realize a lower effective price for the same gas. The following examples will demonstrate this phenomenon.

Example of Buying EFP and
Fixing the Effective Purchase Price

Using EFPs to lock in a fixed price of a physical purchase is a common method whereby end users pay fixed prices for their supply needs. Let's assume XYZ end user is interested in buying one contract/d (10,000 MMBtu/d) on EPNG at Permian for June as an EFP for the purpose of locking in a fixed price purchase for its physical gas supply requirements. In the OTC market, XYZ discovers that FJS producing company is interested in selling a June Permian EFP. After negotiating the EFP differential, XYZ and FJS agree to a differential of minus $0.30. In addition, XYZ and FJS set the EFP posted price at $2.00. At this point, XYZ has two positions to contend with—long June physical gas in Permian (which it already has a requirement to fill) and short June futures contracts. Figure 4.24a illustrates the transaction.

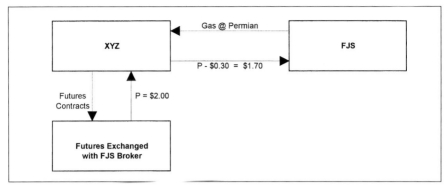

Fig. 4.24a Buying EFP and Fixing Effective Purchase Price

This schedule of payments and receipts shows the relationship between the effective price XYZ pays for its purchase and the invoice price it will pay to FJS.

Pay invoice price (–)	$1.70 (posted price plus differential)
Transfer futures out (+)	$2.00 (posted price)
Futures bought (–)	X
Net purchase price =	($2.00 – X) – $1.70, or
=	- $1.70 + $2.00 – X, or
=	$0.30 – X

The effective purchase price will be a negative number, algebraically, because it represents negative cash flow (cost) to the end user. For simplicity, the negative sign has been dropped from the effective prices in the following discussion.

As you can see, the effective (net) purchase price paid by XYZ depends on the price of the short futures position, which has been transferred into its account from FJS's futures account, is ultimately covered by buying futures contracts. The price for which the futures are bought, dictating the effective purchase price, is left entirely up to XYZ (depending, of course, on where the futures market is trading). For example, if futures are trading $2.45 and XYZ pays $2.45 for 30 June futures to cover the short position in its account, the effective purchase price paid by XYZ for the EFP would be $2.15 (i.e., $2.00 - $2.45 - $1.70 = - $2.15, drop negative sign for simplicity). If, however, futures are trading $1.90 and XYZ pays $1.90 for the 30 June futures to cover the short position in its account, the effective purchase price paid by XYZ for the EFP would only be $1.60 (i.e., $2.00 - $1.70 - $1.90 = - $1.60, drop negative sign for simplicity). This example demonstrates the fact that XYZ can set the effective fixed price for the physical gas in the EFP on its own, depending on where futures are trading and at what price it closes out its short futures position.

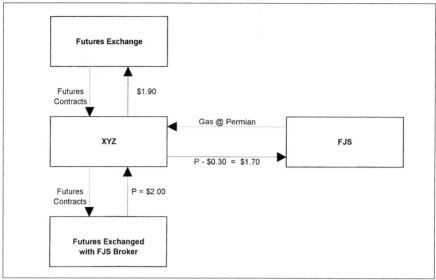

Fig. 4.24b Buying EFP and Fixing Effective Purchase Price

Selling EFP and Fixing the Effective Sale Price

Using EFPs to lock in a fixed price for a physical sale is a common method whereby producers sell supply at fixed prices. Assume FJS producing company is interested in selling one contract/d (10,000 MMBtu/d) of its production at Permian for June as an EFP for the purpose of locking in a fixed price sale. In the OTC market, FJS discovers that XYZ end user is interested in buying a Permian EFP for June. After negotiating the EFP differential, FJS and XYZ agree to set the differential at minus $0.30. In addition, FJS and XYZ set the EFP posted price at $2.00. At this point, FJS has two positions to contend with—short physical June gas in Permian (for which it already has production to cover), and long June futures contracts. Figure 4.25a illustrates the transaction at this point.

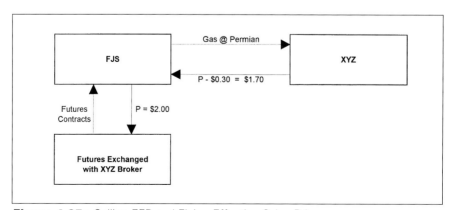

Figure 4.25a Selling EFP and Fixing Effective Sales Price

The following schedule of payments and receipts shows the relationship between the effective price FJS receives from its sale and the invoice price it receives.

Receive invoice price (+) $1.70 (posted price plus differential)
Transfer futures in (-) $2.00 (posted price)
Futures sold (+) X

Net sale price = (X − $2.00) + $1.70, or
 = X − $0.30

The effective (net) sale price realized by FJS depends on the price at which the futures, which have been transferred into its account from XYZ's account, are ultimately sold. The price at which the futures are sold, which dictates the effective sale price therefore, is left up to FJS (depending, of course, on where the futures market is trading). For example, if futures are trading $2.45 and FJS sells the 30 June futures in its account at $2.45, the effective sale price realized by FJS for the EFP would be $2.15 (i.e., $1.70 − $2.00 + 2.45 = $2.15). If, however, futures are trading $1.90 and FJS sells the 30 June futures in its account at $1.90, the effective sale price realized by FJS for the EFP would only be $1.60 (i.e. $1.70 − $2.00 + $1.90 = $1.60) (Fig. 4.25b). Although $1.60 is a lower effective sale price than $1.70 (invoice price), the point is that FJS can make the decision on its own, depending on where futures are trading, as to what effective sale price it will realize from the EFP sale.

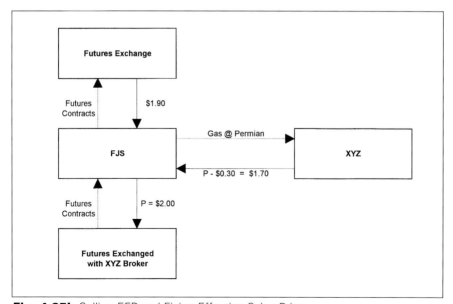

Fig. 4.25b Selling EFP and Fixing Effective Sales Price

Relationship Between
Posted Price and Effective Price

The posted price is of little importance to the ultimate effective price in any EFP transaction. To demonstrate how the agreed upon posted price has no impact on the effective price, let's assume the posted price of the EFP purchased by FJS in the above example was set at $500.00. Refer to this schedule of payments and receipts below.

Receive invoice price (+)	$499.70 (posted price plus differential)
Transfer futures in (X)	$500.00 (posted price)
Futures sold (+)	X
Net sale price	X - $0.30

The effective (net) sale price is still determined by the price at which the futures, which have been transferred into its account from XYZ's account, are ultimately sold. Again, if futures are trading at $2.45 and FJS sells the 30 June futures at $2.45, the effective sale price realized by FJS would still be $2.15 (i.e., $499.70 – $500.00 + $2.45 = $2.15). Likewise, if futures are trading at $1.90 and FJS sells the 30 June futures in its account at $1.90, the effective sale price realized by FJS would still be $1.60 (i.e. $499.70 – $500.00 + $1.90 = $1.60).

The only reason the posted price might be of importance to EFP traders is because of margin requirements by a futures exchange. Futures exchanges require an initial margin (money deposited with the exchange) when opening a futures position. In addition, if the open position deteriorates in value beyond the initial margin amount, the exchange issues a margin call for the amount of that difference. For this reason, many EFP traders are reluctant to agree to a posted price which is not close to the current futures price. What is more common, however, is to delay setting the posted price until a week or so before expiration of that futures contract month. This is almost always the case when long-term EFP transactions are done, primarily so that neither party will be subject to margin calls as futures prices change during the course of the tenure of the EFP.

Timing EFP Trade and Futures Trade

The order in which an EFP is transacted and the futures trade which accompanies it (either buying or selling) does not necessarily have to be in specific order. That is, the EFP can be done first, followed by the futures trade, or vice versa. For example, if a trader speculates that fixed-prices at a location other than the futures contract delivery point will fall, the trader can first initiate a short futures position by selling futures, followed by an EFP sale at that location at a later time or date before expiration (unless making delivery at the futures contract delivery point, which would not require an EFP). As such, the trader already knows the futures price at which the contracts (those that will be transferred into his or her account from the EFP buyers) have been sold, and the only variable left that will determine the effective sale price received is the EFP differential negotiated with the EFP buyer. The opposite can be done in the case where a trader believes prices will rise at a location other than the futures contract delivery point. That is, through first initiating a long futures position by buying futures, then buying an EFP at that location at a later time or date before expiration, the effective price paid for the EFP by the trader is simply the price paid for the futures contracts, plus the EFP differential.

Basis Risk in EFP Trades

From the point of view of switching the order of an EFP transaction and its accompanying futures trade, it should be more clear how the EFP differential received or paid in the EFP transaction can be just as important as the futures price received or paid in the futures trade. EFPs have inherent basis risk in them.

Let's suppose that at a given time, FJS trading company takes a look at the futures market and the Permian EFP market and observes the following prices—futures at $2.00 and Permian EFP differential at minus $0.25.

FJS calculates that at this time, by paying $2.00 for futures and minus $0.25 for an EFP, it could lock-in fixed-price physical gas in the Permian for $1.75 However, instead of buying both the futures and the EFP, FJS just pays $2.00 for futures.

The following day, FJS wants to buy a Permian EFP because it needs fixed price physical gas at that location. FJS takes another look at the futures market and the Permian EFP market and observes the following prices— futures at $2.15 and Permian EFP Differential at minus $0.20.

Because it has already initiated a long futures position in its futures account, which incidentally has made money at this point, FJS is only concerned with the EFP differential it has to pay to fix the price for physical gas in the Permian. The futures contracts will be transferred to the EFP seller's account at the posted price. When FJS calculates its effective purchase price after paying minus $0.20 for the EFP, FJS discovers it will effectively be paying $1.80 for fixed-price physical gas in Permian, as opposed to $1.75 which it could have locked in the previous day. In effect, fixed prices for Permian physical gas (as reflected in the change in the EFP differential) have risen $0.05 more than the futures price. If you recall, this is known as basis risk, and will be addressed in some of the sections that follow.

This chapter has illustrated the flexibility in buying or selling physical gas at fixed prices using EFPs. And more specifically, it has shown how EFPs allow the buyer and seller to independently establish effective fixed prices at their own discretion, subject to futures market prices. It is this feature which contributes most to the popularity of EFPs as a common pricing structure used in trading physical natural gas. The sections below explore the many other ways in which EFPs are used to trade natural gas as well as hedge various forms of other risks in natural gas transactions.

Converting EFPs Into Other Trading Instruments

By combining an EFP with other natural gas trading instruments, its characteristics can be altered such that it may be used to hedge other natural gas transactions (both physical and financial) at various pricing structures. This section will demonstrate how an EFP position can be converted into the following positions—physical index gas, physical fixed-price gas, basis swap, and a futures swap.

If you recall, an EFP position is essentially a package of other trading instruments. More specifically, an EFP is composed of physical gas at index, a basis swap, and futures contracts.

Therefore, if any of main components are stripped out from the EFP position, the EFP can take on the characteristics of another trading instrument. This is another reason why EFPs are such a popular trading tool.

Converting an EFP Into Physical Index Gas. To convert an EFP into physical index gas, we need to strip out both the basis swap position and the futures contract position. For example, if we are paying posted price minus $0.25 for a Permian EFP, we are effectively paying L3D minus $0.25 for a Permian basis swap, paying Permian index for the physical gas in Permian, and selling futures contracts at L3D. Therefore, if we sell a Permian basis swap at L3D minus $0.25, and pay L3D for futures contracts, we are essentially left with a long physical Permian index gas position. Figures 4.26a,b and c show the stages of conversion from an EFP to physical index gas:

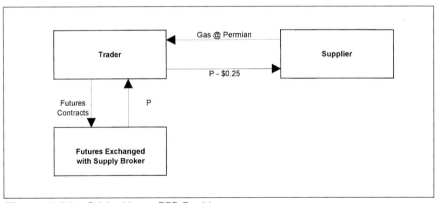

Figure 4.26a Original Long EFP Position

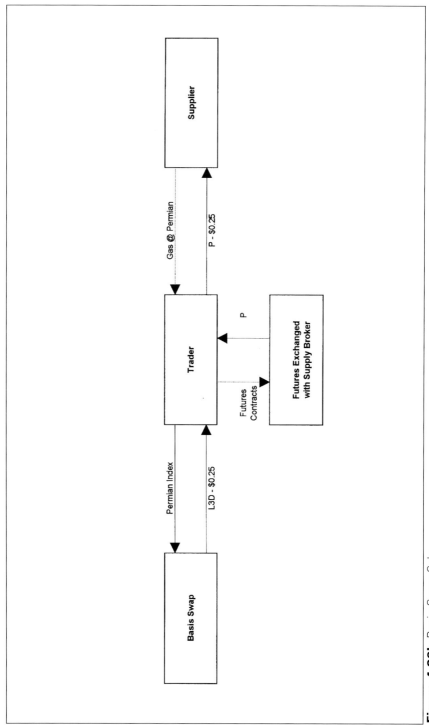

Figure 4.26b Basis Swap Sale

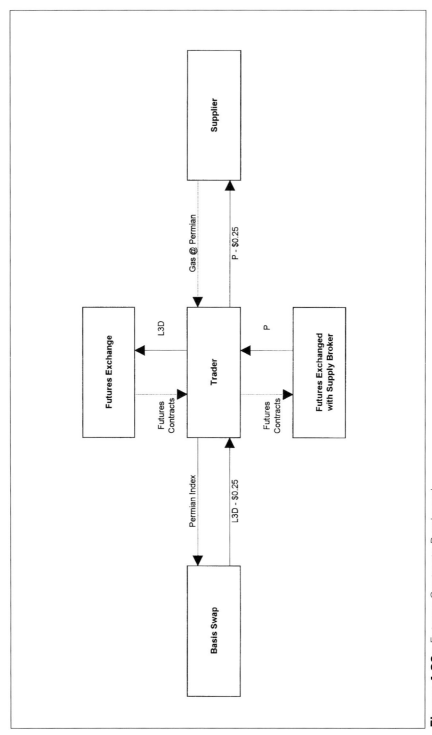

Figure 4.26c Futures Contracts Purchased

A schedule of payments and receipts summarizing the net effective purchase price of the EFP once all steps have been completed follows.

Pay EFP invoice price (–)   P + (- $0.25) (posted price plus differential)
Transfer EFP futures out (+) P   (posted price)
Pay to basis swap (–)   Index
Receive from basis swap (+) L3D - $0.25
Futures bought (–)   L3D

Effective purchase price   Index

By isolating the gain from the first part of the transaction (plus $0.25) and isolating the loss from the receive from basis swap, futures bought part of the transaction (minus $0.25), the two cancel each other out, resulting in a payment of index.

By paying P minus $0.25 for an EFP and subsequently selling a basis swap at L3D minus $0.25, and paying L3D for futures contracts to liquidate the given short position, the outcome is a long physical index gas position valued at index flat. In this example, we are assuming that the EFP differential is the same as the basis swap differential. What would happen, however, if the two were not equal? The resulting value of index gas after a hedge (or conversion) has been done is affected by the difference, if any, between the two fixed-price legs in the trade (the fixed-price leg in a basis swap is the component). Similar rules apply to accounting for change in value of Index when trading EFPs with basis swaps as those when trading fixed-price physical gas with fixed-float index swaps:

When *buying* an EFP and selling a basis swap to hedge, simply add the difference between the differential paid for the EFP versus the differential received from the basis swap to Index if it is a negative difference, or subtract the difference between the differential paid for the EFP versus the differential received from the basis swap from Index if it is a positive difference.

For example:
1. Pay – $0.25 for EFP, sell basis swap at – $0.20 = long gas at index – $0.05,
2. Pay – $0.25 for EFP, sell basis swap at – $0.25 = long gas at index flat,
3. Pay – $0.25 for EFP, sell basis swap at - $0.30 = long gas at index + $0.05.

When *selling* an EFP and buying a basis swap to hedge, simply subtract the difference between the differential received from the EFP versus the differential paid for the basis swap from index if it is a negative difference, or add the difference between the differential received from the EFP versus the differential paid for the basis swap to Index if it is a positive difference.

For example:
1. Sell EFP at – $0.25, pay - $0.30 for basis swap = short gas at Index + $0.05,
2. Sell EFP at – $0.25, pay – $0.25 for basis swap = short gas at index flat,
3. Sell EFP at – $0.25, pay – $0.20 for basis swap = short gas at Index – $0.05.

By offsetting an EFP position with a basis swap, a trader can effectively initiate an index position, or hedge an existing index position.

Converting an EFP Into Fixed-Price Physical Gas. To convert an EFP into fixed-price physical gas, we need to strip out only the futures contract position. For example, if we are paying posted price minus $0.25 for a Permian EFP, we are effectively paying L3D minus $0.25 for a Permian basis swap, paying Permian index for the physical gas in Permian, and selling futures contracts at L3D. Therefore, if we pay a fixed price instead of L3D for the futures contracts, we have fixed the price of that physical gas at the price paid for the futures contracts, plus or minus the EFP differential, and are long physical gas at that fixed price.

Converting an EFP Into a Basis Swap. To convert an EFP into a basis swap, we need to strip out both the physical index gas position and the futures contract position. For example, if we are paying posted price minus $0.25 for a Permian EFP, are effectively paying L3D minus $0.25 for a Permian basis swap, paying Permian index for the physical gas in Permian, and selling futures contracts at L3D. Therefore, if we sell the physical gas in Permian at Index, and pay L3D for the futures contracts, we will be left with a long Permian basis swap position valued at L3D minus $0.25. Figures 4.27a, b, and c show the stages of conversion from an EFP to a basis swap.

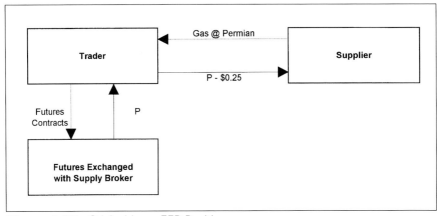

Figure 4.27a Original Long EFP Position

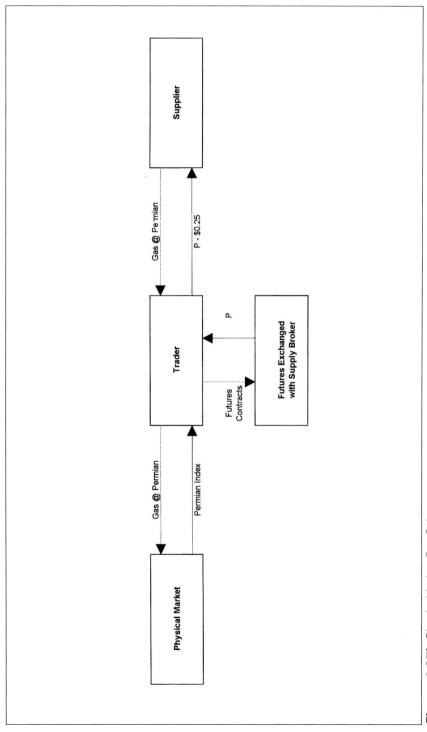

Figure 4.27b Physical Index Gas Sale

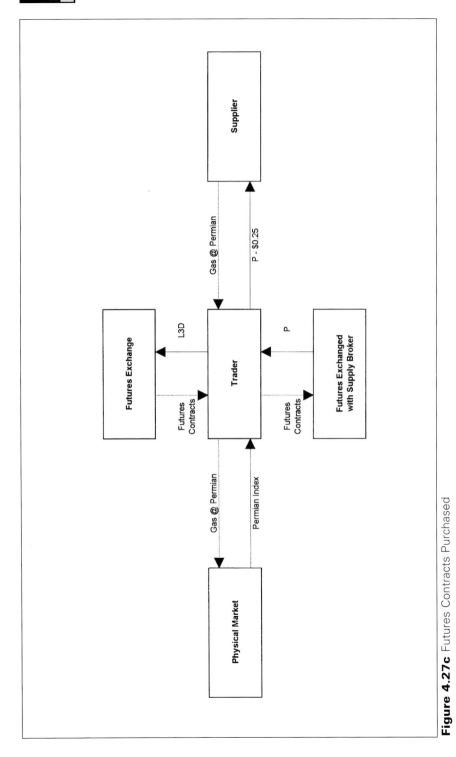

Figure 4.27c Futures Contracts Purchased

Here is a schedule of payments and receipts summarizing the effective basis swap position once all steps have been completed.

Pay EFP invoice price (−) P + (− $0.25) (posted price plus differential)
Transfer EFP futures out (+) P   (posted price)
Receive from index sale (+) Index
Futures bought (−) L3D

Effective position Receive $0.25
                    Receive index
                    Pay L3D

By applying the gain from the first part of the transaction (plus $0.25) to the price paid for futures (L3D) by subtracting it from the cost, the result is effectively a long Permian basis swap position because we pay L3D minus $0.25 and receive Permian index.

Therefore, by paying P minus $0.25 for an EFP and subsequently selling the physical gas in Permian at Permian index flat, and paying L3D for futures contracts to liquidate the given short position, the outcome is a long Permian basis swap position valued at L3D minus $0.25. Therefore, an EFP trader is able to hedge a basis swap position in a way other than with an outright basis swap Although it seems that simply buying or selling a basis swap outright would be an easier and more efficient means of creating or closing a basis swap position, there are times when a better effective basis swap differential can be achieved through using an EFP and stripping out the index gas. These are also arbitrage opportunities for EFP and basis swap traders similar to the arbitraging of fixed-float index swaps.

In the previous example, we assumed that the physical gas in Permian was sold at index flat. What would happen to the effective outcome of the hedge, if the physical gas were sold at either a discount or a premium to index? The outcome is more straightforward than you might think. The resulting value of the basis swap after stripping out the physical index gas and liquidating the given futures position from an EFP trade is affected by the difference, if any, between index and the actual price received or paid when selling or buying the index gas, respectively. The same methodology applies when accounting for the value of a basis swap after stripping out the index gas from an EFP as in trading fixed-price physical gas with fixed-float index swaps.

When buying an EFP and selling the index gas, simply add the difference between index and the actual index sale price received for the physical gas to the basis swap differential if it is a negative difference, or subtract the difference between the index and the actual index sale price received for the physical gas from the basis swap differential if it is a positive difference.

For examples:
1. Pay –$0.25 for EFP, sell gas at Index - $0.05 = long basis swap at L3D –$0.20,
2. Pay –$0.25 for EFP, sell gas at Index "flat" = long basis swap at L3D – $0.25
3. Pay –$0.25 for EFP, sell gas at Index + $0.05 = long basis swap at L3D – $0.30.

When selling an EFP and buying the index gas, simply subtract the difference between index and the actual index price paid for the physical gas from the basis swap differential if it is a negative difference, or add the difference between the index and the actual index price paid for the physical gas to the basis swap differential if it is a positive difference.

For examples:
1. Sell EFP at – $0.25, pay index + $0.05 for gas = short basis swap at L3D – $0.30,
2. Sell EFP at – $0.25, pay index flat for gas = short basis swap at L3D – $0.25,
3. Sell EFP at - $0.25, pay index – $0.05 for gas = short basis swap at L3D – $0.20.

Converting an EFP Into a Futures Swap. To convert an EFP into a futures swap (no physical gas, no basis), we need to strip out both the physical index gas position and the basis swap position. For example, if we are paying posted price minus $0.25 for a Permian EFP, we are effectively paying L3D minus $0.25 for a Permian basis swap, paying Permian index for the physical gas in Permian, and selling futures contracts at L3D. Therefore, if we sell the physical gas in Permian at index, sell a Permian basis swap at L3D minus $0.25, and pay $2.00 for futures contracts, we will be left with a long futures swap position valued at $2.00 versus LTD. Figures 4.28a, b, c, and d show the stages of conversion from an EFP to a futures swap follow.

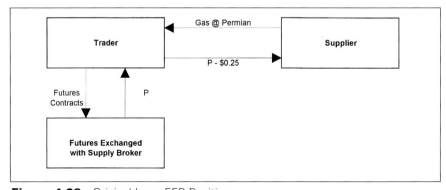

Figure 4.28a Original Long EFP Position

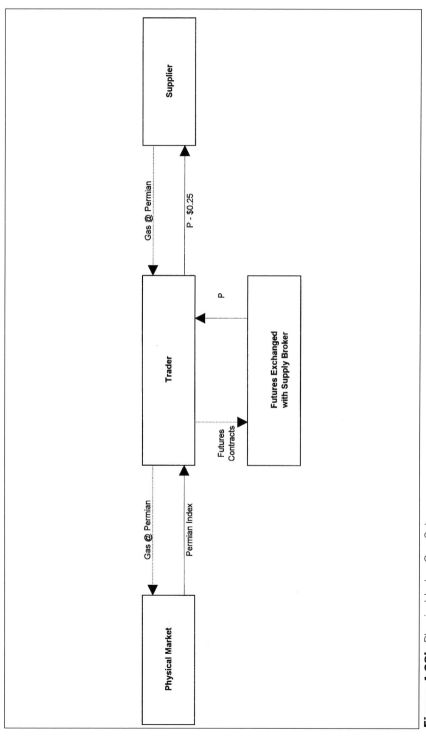

Figure 4.28b Physical Index Gas Sale

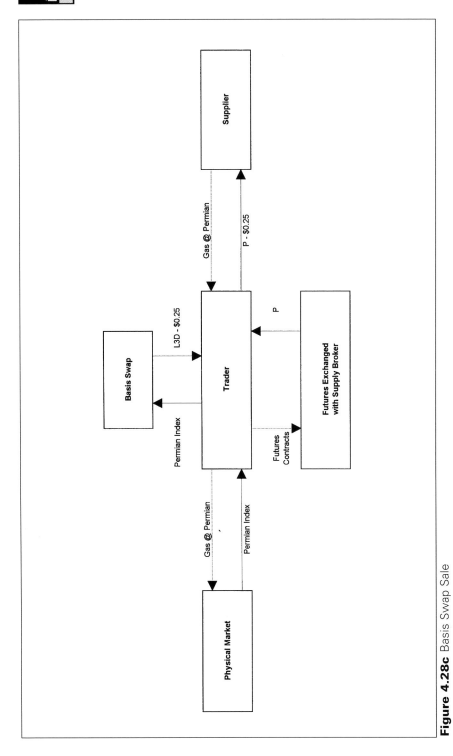

Figure 4.28c Basis Swap Sale

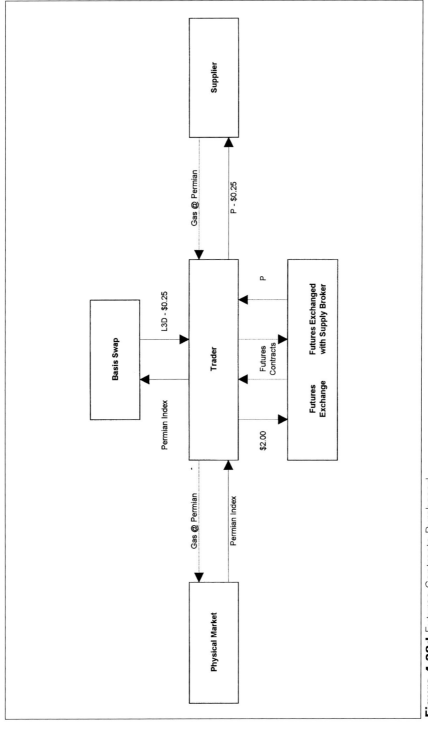

Figure 4.28d Futures Contracts Purchased

The schedule of payments and receipts below summarizes the effective futures swap position once all steps have been completed.

Pay EFP Invoice Price (−)   P + (− $0.25) (posted price plus differential)
Transfer EFP futures out (+) P   (posted price)
Receive from index sale (+)   Index
Pay to basis swap (−)   Index
Receive from basis swap (+)   L3D − $0.25
Futures bought (−) $2.00

Effective position   Receive $0.25
                             Receive L3D − $0.25
                             Pay $2.00

or equivalently   Pay $2.00
                            Receive L3D

By applying the gain from the first part of the transaction (plus $0.25) to the price received from the basis swap (L3D minus $0.25), the result is effectively a $2.00 long futures swap position (i.e., pay $2.00, receive L3D).

Converting an EFP into a Fixed-Float Index Swap. To convert an EFP into an index swap, we need to first convert the EFP into a basis swap, and then add a futures swap to convert into an index swap. Using the same example as above, if we are paying posted price minus $0.25 for a Permian EFP, we are effectively paying L3D minus $0.25 for a Permian basis swap, paying Permian index for the physical gas in Permian, and selling futures contracts at L3D. Therefore, if we sell the physical gas in Permian at index, pay L3D for futures contracts, and pay $2.00 for a futures swap, we will be left with a long Permian index swap position valued at $1.75. Figure 4.29a, b, c, and d show the stages of conversion from an EFP to a fixed float index swap.

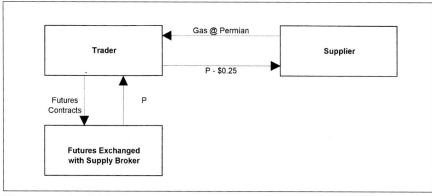

Figure 4.29a Original Long EFP Position

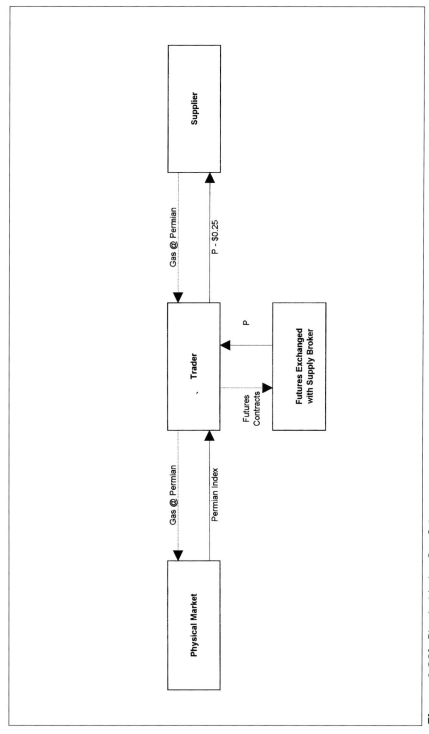

Figure 4.29b Physical Index Gas Sale

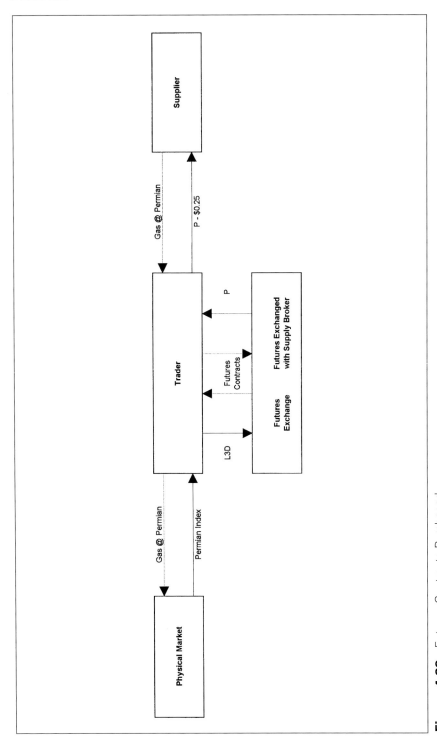

Figure 4.29c Futures Contracts Purchased

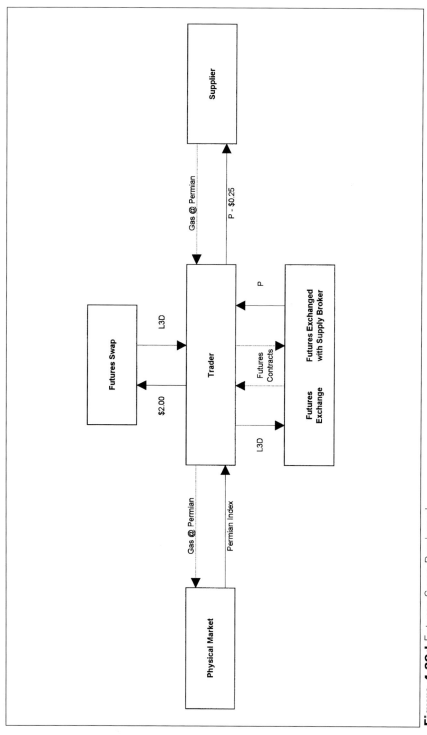

Figure 4.29d Futures Swap Purchased

The following schedule of payments and receipts summarizes the effective Permian index swap position once all steps have been completed.

Pay EFP Invoice Price (−)	P + (− $0.25)	(posted price plus differential)
Transfer EFP futures out (+)	P	(posted price)
Receive from index sale (+)	Index	
Futures bought (−)	L3D	
Receive from futures swap (+)	L3D	
Pay to futures swap (−)	$2.00	
Effective position	Receive $0.25	
	Receive index	
	Pay $2.00	
or equivalently	Pay $1.75	
	Receive index	

By applying the gain from the first part of the transaction (plus $0.25) to the price paid to the futures swap ($2.00), the result is effectively a $1.75 long Permian Index swap position (i.e., pay $1.75, receive index).

EFP Summary

EFPs are a valuable natural gas trading tool because of the many ways in which they can be combined with other natural gas trading instruments to hedge, and/or speculate on, physical and financial positions, basis swaps, futures swaps, and index swaps. More specifically, the mechanics of an EFP enable the buyer and the seller to independently control the effective pricing and intended purpose of the instrument. EFPs should therefore be included in every natural gas trader's repertoire of available hedging and speculating tools.

Triggers

Definition

In the natural gas market, *a trigger* is a form of pricing which is a hybrid of EFP pricing. Unlike an EFP, where effective pricing by both buyer and seller is done independently, a trigger requires notification by one party of its intent to trigger, or fix, the effective price. In other words, a trigger is a physical transaction priced at a differential to a futures contract where the price can be locked in by one party through the addition of a futures swap executed at a later date with the other party. Trigger deadlines vary from any time previous to the third-to-last futures trading day, to as late as half an hour before expiration of the futures contract. The most common deadline is prior to the third-to-last futures trading day, and if this deadline passes, the triggering party's default effective price is L3D plus or minus the differential. The party granting the right to trigger is exposed to no risk different from that in a normal EFP trade.

Components and Properties of a Trigger

Initially, a trigger consists of two components—a basis swap, and physical gas valued at index. When the effective price is set, triggered, a futures swap is added to the initial transaction. The trigger customer typically does the futures swap with the same party as it did the physical component of the trade with, although a third party could be used, simply letting the physical trade component in the trigger be priced under the default pricing established. The effective price to the trigger customer will still be the same. A long trigger equals a long basis swap and, long gas at index, and a short trigger equals a short basis swap and, short gas at index.

The components of a trigger are nearly identical to those of an EFP with the exception of the given futures contract positions in an EFP. Therefore, a trader that is buying a trigger is essentially buying a basis swap for a particular location, and buying index gas at that same location. Likewise, a trader that is selling a trigger is essentially selling a basis swap for a particular location, and selling index gas at that same location.

As a result of the similarities to EFPs, triggers can be hedged and traded in practically the same ways. If a trader is long a trigger, he or she could sell a basis swap and be left long physical Index gas. Or, if the trader needed to be long a basis swap, he or she could sell the physical index gas. In this sense, a trigger is simply a package of physical index gas coupled with a basis swap. When the trigger is elected (thereby setting the effective fixed price), a futures swap is simply added to the equation as a separate transaction.

The reader is probably wondering why anyone would enter into a trigger instead of an EFP transaction, or buying or selling physical index gas and a basis swap. There may be other reasons, but the most common is that many market participants still have not opened futures trading accounts. To accommodate these types of customers, several trading companies, producers, and end users will agree on a differential with a customer and allow that customer to trigger and set the effective fixed price for the gas at the customer's discretion. Of course, the process of triggering requires that the customer contact the trader during trading hours, prior to the specified trigger deadline, and enter into a futures swap with that trader to lock in the effective price. Because of the obvious administrative hassles in granting customers this luxury, many traders will make it worth their while by scalping both the differential for the physical gas and the fixed price of the futures swap.

Hedging Trigger Sale with an EFP

Let's suppose that FJS trading company has a customer looking for a Permian trigger. The customer does not have a futures account, but would still like to price its supply based on the futures market. FJS is more than willing to accommodate its customers needs, and therefore agrees to sell a trigger to its customer. Because triggers are traded in much the same way as EFPs (although the customer will not be transferring futures into FJS's account), FJS decides to hedge the trigger sale to its customer by buying an EFP in the market. FJS obtains the market for Permian EFPs and discovers that it can buy one for minus $0.27. FJS relays a minus $0.25 offer for a Permian trigger to its customer, and the customer accepts the deal, with the provision that the customer triggers no later than the close of trading on the fourth-to-last futures trading day for that contract month. To hedge the trigger sale, FJS pays minus $0.27 for the Permian EFP. Figure 4.30a illustrates the two transactions for FJS up to this point follows.

What positions, if any, does FJS currently have? From a physical standpoint, FJS has no position because it is covering the physical trigger sale to its customer in the Permian with a Permian EFP. However, FJS does have a short futures position valued at L3D because it must transfer out futures contracts to the EFP seller's account in exchange for the physical gas in the Permian under the EFP agreement. If the customer triggers before the deadline, FJS will then need to buy either futures or a futures swap to hedge its fixed-price risk when the customer sets its effective price.

The following week (still before the deadline), the customer sees the futures contract on his screen trading $2.25 (a good price), and calls FJS to trigger and set its effective price for the Permian physical gas under the trigger arrangement. Since FJS is already short futures contracts at L3D because it has bought an EFP, FJS should use futures contracts to hedge the futures swap it will sell to its trigger customer. Therefore, after calling its broker and obtaining a $2.24 bid at $2.25 market for futures, FJS offers its trigger customer a futures swap at $2.255. Since the trigger customer realizes that FJS is providing a service and that the customer should pay for the trigger service, the trigger customer agrees to pay $2.255 for the futures swap, thereby locking in an effective price in the Permian of $2.005 for physical gas (i.e., $2.255 − $0.25 = $2.005). FJS gives the buy order to its broker and is filled at a better price of $2.245, and the transaction is complete. Fig. 4.30b shows the completed transaction and the schedule of payments and receipts below shows the total profit on the trade for FJS.

Pay EFP Invoice Price (−)	P + (− $0.27)	(posted price plus differential)
Transfer EFP futures out (+)	P	(posted price)
Receive from trigger sale (+)	$2.005	
Futures bought (−)	$2.245	
Profit / loss on trade	$0.03 x number of contracts	

By applying the gain from the first part of the transaction (plus $0.27) to the price paid to the loss between futures bought and receive from trigger sale ($0.24), the result is a $0.03 profit.

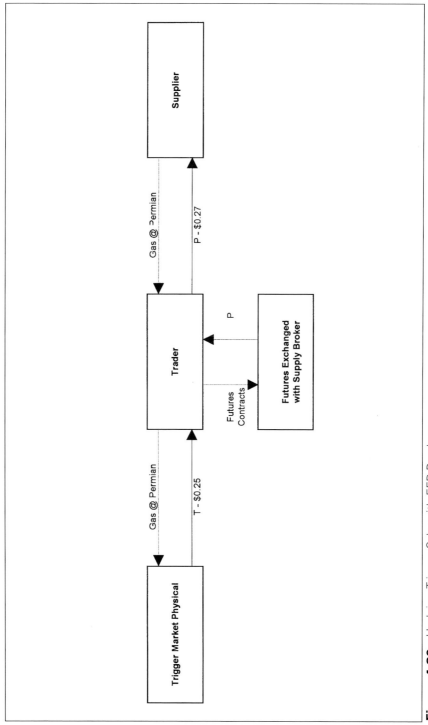

Figure 4.30a Hedging Trigger Sale with EFP Purchase

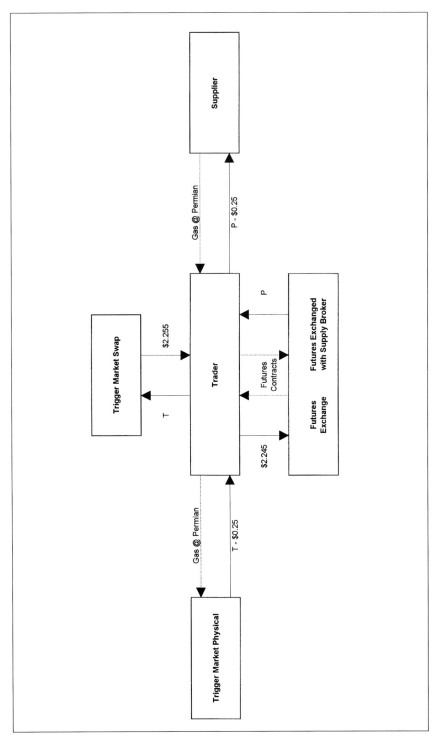

Figure 4.30b Hedging "Triggered" Sale by Buying Futures

Another way of accounting for the payments and receipts for FJS is to treat the two components (physical trigger sale and futures swap with trigger customer) as two separate trades.

Pay EFP Invoice Price (–)   P + (– $0.27) (posted price plus differential)
Transfer EFP futures out (+)   P   (posted price)
Receive from trigger sale (+)   L3D – $0.25 (L3D is default trigger)
Pay to futures swap (–)   L3D
Receive from futures swap (+) $2.255
Futures bought (–) $2.245

Profit /loss on trade $0.03 x number of contracts

When the futures swap is added to the transaction, it effectively replaces the default trigger price (L3D) with the triggered fixed price. Therefore, once the customer has triggered, or after the deadline when L3D is known, it is easiest to write up the trade as a fixed-price physical trade at the effective Permian price instead of writing up another trade as a futures swap. This saves administrative time and money.

Hedging Trigger Sale with Physical Index Gas

The previous example demonstrates how most triggers are typically hedged. However, the position could have just as effectively been hedged with index gas instead of an EFP. Here's an example of how FJS could have hedged the Permian trigger sale at minus $0.25 with physical index gas already in its portfolio. Figure 4.31a shows the transaction up to this point.

FJS has basis risk as the profit or loss on the trade depends on what the actual basis differential of Permian to futures actually is. In addition, if the customer triggers, FJS will need to buy (because FJS will be effectively selling at a fixed price after the trigger) either a futures swap, or actual futures contracts. For this example, we will assume FJS will use actual futures contracts and successfully liquidate at L3D, although a futures swap would eliminate L3D risk. Therefore, to hedge its basis risk, FJS pays L3D minus $0.27 for a Permian basis swap (assume same differential as EFP in above example). The next diagram shows how the transaction would look after FJS buys the Permian basis swap.

At this point, the trigger sale has been completely hedged, both physically and financially. If the customer let the trigger price default (L3D), FJS would not have to do anything more with this transaction, other than count the money it made ($0.02 times the number of contracts). However, the customer sees the futures contract trading $2.25, and calls FJS to trigger and set its effective price for the Permian physical gas. FJS follows the same steps as in the previous example and the customer's effective Permian price has been set at $2.005. Because FJS is now long futures contracts, it must successfully liquidate them at L3D to match the payment to the basis swap. After doing so,

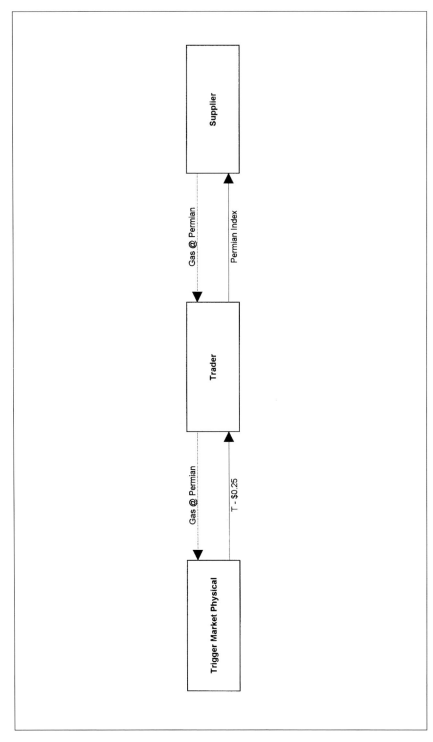

Figure 4.31a, Hedging Trigger Sale with Physical Index Supply

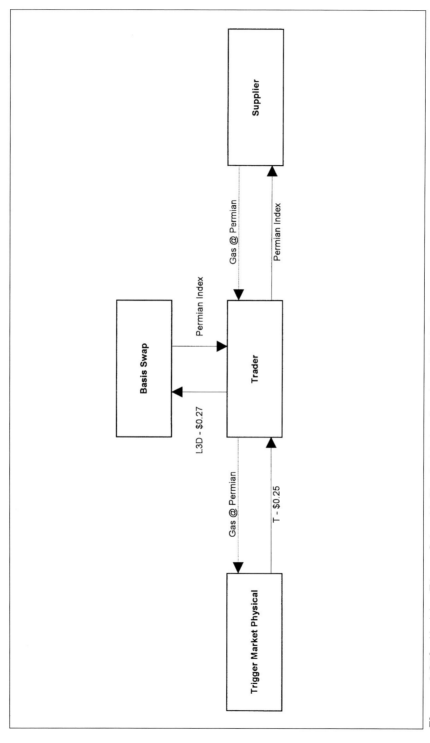

Figure 4.31b. Hedging Trigger Sale with Physical Index Supply and Basis Swap

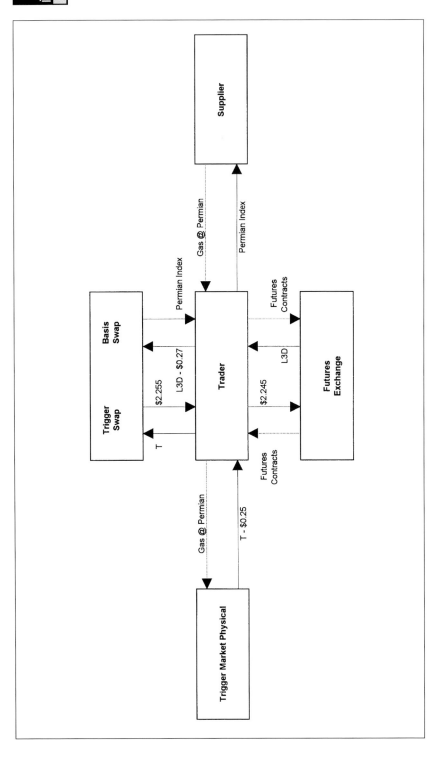

Figure 4.31c. Hedging Triggered Sale by Buying Futures

the transaction is complete, and FJS can count the money it has made ($0.03 times the number of contracts). A final diagram follows which illustrates the completed transaction and the schedule of payments and receipts shows the total profit on the trade.

Receive from trigger sale (+) $2.005
Futures bought (−) $2.245
Futures sold (+)   L3D
Pay to basis swap (−)   L3D − $0.27
Receive from basis swap (+) Index
Pay to supply portfolio (−) Index

Profit / (Loss) on trade $0.03 x number of contracts

If the physical supply in the portfolio, or purchased specifically for this trade, costs more than index flat, this cost must be factored in to what the basis swap differential should be. For example, if the profit margin on the trade is to remain at $0.03, but index gas costs index plus $0.01, the basis swap differential would need to be L3D minus $0.28 to cover this additional $0.01 cost to maintain the $0.03 profit.

Although triggers are most effectively hedged with an EFP, the first hedge to be made should always be one which converts the trigger purchase or sale into an index purchase or sale via a basis swap. This is because indexes are less volatile than basis differentials, and if the basis market should change between the time a trigger purchase or sale is made and an EFP is sold or bought to hedge, the trader is more at risk of losing money than if the trigger was first converted into an index transaction then covered with an EFP and basis swap combination at a later time.

Hedging Trigger Sale with Fixed-Price Physical Gas

The trigger sale in the example above could also have been hedged with fixed-price physical gas. The following is an example of how FJS could have hedged the Permian trigger sale at minus $0.25 with fixed-price physical gas. Figure 4.32a shows the transaction up to this point.

This trade has both basis risk and fixed-price risk. The best way to approach hedging a trade like this if it can't be hedged with an EFP is to hedge one risk at a time. Since FJS hasn't bought the gas at a fixed price up to this point, it is only exposed to basis risk. That is, if the Permian basis to futures tightens before FJS can buy fixed-price gas, FJS will be stuck with a trigger sale that is below market. To avoid this, let's assume FJS is able to pay L3D minus $0.27 for a Permian basis swap. The next diagram shows how this transaction is added to the puzzle.

Now that the basis risk is hedged, FJS has essentially converted the trigger sale price into index plus $0.02.

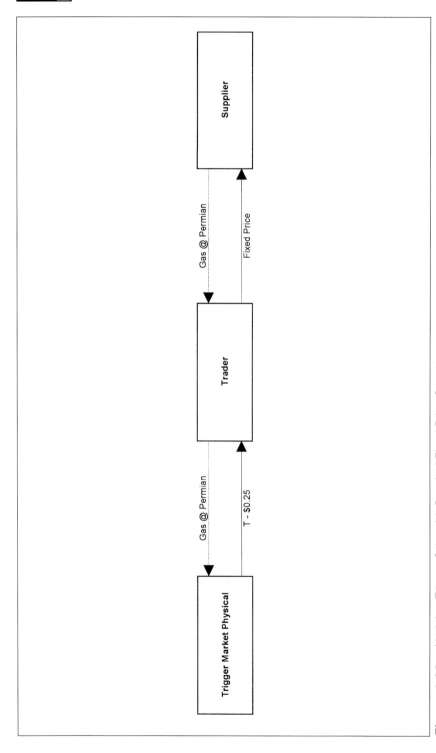

Figure 4.32a. Hedging Trigger Sale with Physical Fixed-Price Supply

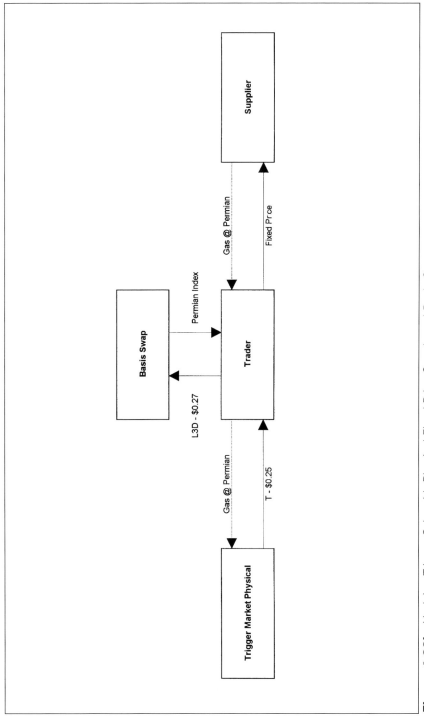

Figure 4.32b. Hedging Trigger Sale with Physical Fixed-Price Supply and Basis Swap

Now that FJS can focus on buying the physical gas at a fixed price (which will have to be swapped into index), what fixed price should FJS target when trying to buy physical gas in the market? It depends on either the bid for the Permian fixed float index swap or the bid for both the Permian basis swap and futures. Let's suppose that the bid for a Permian index swap is $2.00, but that the bid for a Permian basis swap is L3D minus $0.25 and the bid for futures is $2.26. Since the effective Permian fixed float index swap bid, calculated by packaging the basis swap and futures together (i.e., $2.26 - $0.25 = $2.01), is better than the outright Permian fixed float index swap bid ($2.00), FJS targets $2.00 as a fixed price to buy physical gas in hopes of making another $0.01 on the trade by selling both the basis swap and futures. However, FJS will at least retain the profit already made if it must resort to hitting the outright $2.00 index swap bid if the package falls apart before FJS can trade it. For simplicity, let's assume FJS is able to pay $2.00 for physical gas in the Permian, and that it is able to sell both the Permian basis swap at L3D minus $0.25 and futures at $2.26.

Again, at this point, the trade is completely hedged. If the customer calls to trigger and thereby set its effective fixed price in the Permian, FJS would simply obtain the offer in the futures market, add any additional profit it feels it could make on the trade, relay its trigger offer to the customer, and, if the customer wants to trigger, FJS would buy back the futures that it is short, and completely close out the trade. Now the reader can see why it is so much easier to hedge a trigger purchase or sale with an EFP.

The final schedule of payments and receipts for FJS follows showing the total profit on the trade (assume customer triggers at $2.255, FJS pays $2.245 for the futures to hedge).

Receive from market (+)	L3D – $0.25	(gas sale to trigger customer)
Pay to basis swap (–)	L3D – $0.27	
Receive from basis swap (+)	Index	
Pay to supply (–)	$2.00	
Futures sold (+)	$2.26	
Receive from basis swap (+)	L3D – $0.26	
Pay to basis swap (–)	Index	
Pay to futures swap (–)	L3D	(swap with trigger customer)
Receive from futures swap (+)	$2.255	(swap with trigger customer)
Futures bought (–)	$2.245	
Profit /loss on trade	$0.043 x number of contracts	

Triggers are still a common way of transacting for physical gas by many market participants. Triggers are usually requested by those companies that are not set up with, a futures trading account of their own. It seems ironic that these companies are permitted to trade physical gas based on a floating futures price (trigger), which merely relocates their fixed-price risk from the

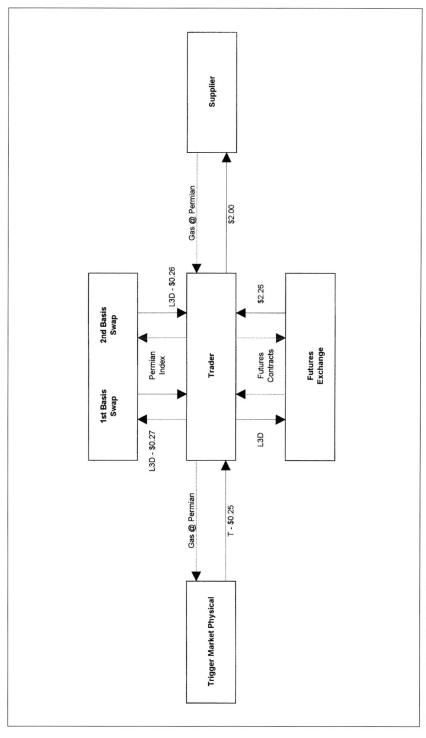

Figure 4.32c. Hedging Trigger Sale with Physical Fixed-Price Supply, Basis Swaps, & Futures

futures contract delivery point to an alternate delivery point, yet they are not permitted to take fixed-price positions using futures. Trigger customers usually afford a profitable trading opportunity to those traders who can facilitate their requests, and still hedge themselves.

Options

Financial Market Definition of Options

An *option contract*, in general, is an agreement between two parties giving the buyer of the option the right, but not the obligation, to purchase or sell a given commodity or security at a specified price at any time up to and including the expiration of the option contract. Options are another type of financial trading instrument used to manage risk and or speculate in the natural gas market as well as other commodities and securities markets. Natural gas options (and most other options on commodities) are traded on the futures exchanges (usually in close proximity to the futures trading area) as well as in the OTC market, and have increasingly become more actively traded due to the volatility in the natural gas market.

Types of Options Contracts

There are two types of options—calls and puts. A *call option* grants the buyer of the option the right, but not the obligation, to buy the underlying commodity or security from the seller of the call option at a specified price (*strike price*) at any time up to and including the expiration of the option. The seller of a call option is, therefore, obligated to sell the underlying commodity or security to the buyer of the call option, at the strike price, at any time up to and including the expiration date. A *put option* grants the buyer of the option the right, but not the obligation, to sell the underlying commodity or security to the seller of the put option at the strike price at any time up to and including the expiration of the option. The seller of a put option is, therefore, obligated to buy the underlying commodity or security from the buyer of the put option at the strike price at any time up to and including the expiration date. The buyer of a call option, therefore, profits if prices rise, and the buyer of a put option profits if prices fall.

Option Risk

For each option, the buyer's risk is limited to what it has paid for the option (*option premium*), but the seller's risk is theoretically unlimited for the duration of the option's life. For example, suppose February natural gas futures are trading $2.05. If FJS pays $0.10 for five February $2.00 calls on natural gas futures to XYZ for a total cost of $5,000, FJS has the right, but not the obligation, to buy five February natural gas futures contracts from XYZ for $2.00 between now and the expiration date of the options contracts.

If February natural gas prices rise to $2.25, FJS will either sell the five Feb $2.00 calls back in the market, if there is still time left before they expire, or exercise them. *Exercising* an option is the process whereby the buyer of an option (either a put or a call) elects to execute its given right to either buy (call) or sell (put) the underlying commodity or security from or to the option seller at the strike price. By exercising its option to buy five February natural gas futures for $2.00 from XYZ, FJS would be made long five February futures contracts which it could either sell at $2.25 for a net profit of $7,500 or take delivery of the physical gas at expiration by not selling the futures contracts. If natural gas prices fall below $2.00, however, FJS will let the calls expire worthless, essentially forfeiting the $5,000 premium it paid for them. Options expire worthless when it would be more economical to buy or sell futures in the market as opposed to exercising the option. For example, if FJS needed to buy February futures (hence the call option), and if February futures were trading $1.90 at expiration of the options, FJS would not exercise its $2.00 calls with XYZ and would instead simply pay $1.90 for futures in the market.

On the other hand, XYZ (the seller of the call options to FJS) is obligated, regardless of how high prices go, to sell five February futures to FJS at any point up to and including the expiration of the options. Therefore, if futures rise to $2.25, FJS would exercise the five February $2.00 calls and XYZ would lose $0.15 (i.e., $2.25 − $2.00 + $0.10) by paying $2.25 for futures, and selling them to FJS at $2.00. However, if prices fall to $1.90, XYZ would keep the $5,000 premium paid to it by FJS. As you can see, the risk to XYZ is not defined but the risk to FJS is limited to the premium it pays for the options.

Hedging Naked Option Risk

As mentioned in the previous example, if February natural gas futures prices rose to $2.25, and FJS exercised its five February $2.00 calls, XYZ would lose the difference between the strike price and the futures price, less the premium it received. This is based on the assumption that XYZ did not hedge its theoretically unlimited exposure to rising prices. In fact, XYZ may have even profited on the trade. It all depends on if, and how, XYZ hedged its short call sale (naked calls) to FJS.

There are many ways both naked and covered option positions can be hedged. In fact, hundreds of options hedging and trading books have been written on the subject due to the complexity and wide variety of hedging and trading techniques with options.

Let's look at two simple scenarios whereby XYZ could have profited from the five February $2.00 call options it wrote (sold) to FJS in the example above. The simplest way to profit from trading options is to adhere to the old adage, "buy low, sell high." Options are traded in much the same way futures, or fixed-price physical commodities, are for that matter. There is usually a bid/offer spread for options with strike prices that surround (either above or below) the price where the actual underlying commodity is trading. The term usually is inserted because option activity depends on how active the particular underlying commodity or security is. If the underlying is more volatile, several strike prices above and below the price of the underlying will be actively quoted and traded. Therefore, if futures were earlier trading $1.85, and XYZ paid $0.05 for five February $2.00 calls because it thought February futures prices would rise (increasing the value of call options), it could have later turned around and sold them to FJS at $0.10 after prices did rise. In this instance, XYZ would have been completely hedged on its call sale to FJS because it had covered with a purchase of the same options. If futures prices rose to $2.25 and FJS exercised its $2.00 calls, XYZ would exercise the $2.00 calls it paid $0.05 for. In fact, XYZ could have even bought five February $1.95 calls for $0.10, sold five February $2.00 calls later to FJS, and still have been covered.

Another option trade, which is also a hedging technique depending on the order in which its done, is known as a covered write. A *covered write* is the process whereby a position in the underlying commodity or security, which has previously been established, is offset with the sale of an option. For example, if XYZ sold five February $2.00 calls at $0.10 to FJS (naked call), and subsequently paid $1.95 for five February natural gas futures contracts (long position), XYZ would have hedged its exposure to rising prices. However, if prices fell below $1.85 (futures price less premium received), and XYZ did not sell the futures contracts back, it would begin to lose money on the futures position as prices fell further. If prices did fall to $1.85, and XYZ sold the futures contracts back, but prices then began to rise, XYZ would again be exposed to an undefined risk of prices above $2.00, with no premium left (due to $0.10 loss on futures trade) to compensate for that risk. Options trading can be very confusing and hazardous to your wealth if the risks and rewards are not properly understood.

Option Valuation

The price of an option is called its premium. The option premium is paid by the buyer to the seller, typically at the time the option contract is written—synonymous with selling. An option's premium value is made up of two components—intrinsic value and time value. *Intrinsic value* is the positive difference, if any, between the strike price of the option, and the price of the underlying commodity or security for which that option is based on. *Time Value* is the remaining value other than intrinsic. In the previous example, because natural gas futures were trading $2.05 when FJS paid $0.10 for the $2.00 calls, they had $0.05 of intrinsic value ($2.05 − $2.00 = $0.05), and $0.05 of time value ($0.10 − $0.05 = $0.05). If futures had subsequently risen to $2.25 and the $2.00 calls were trading $0.32, the option premium would consist of $0.25 of intrinsic value ($2.25 − $2.00 = $0.25), and $0.07 of time value ($0.32 − $0.25 = $0.07).

An option which has intrinsic value is called an *in the money* option. An option whose strike price is equal to or very near the current price of the underlying commodity or security is called an *at the money* option. An option which has no intrinsic value and whose strike price is not equal to or very near the current price of the underlying commodity or security is called an *out of the money* option. For example, if natural gas is trading $2.00, the $1.90 calls and the $2.10 puts are in the money. The $2.00 calls and $2.00 puts are at the money, and the $2.10 calls and the $1.90 puts are out of the money.

In general, the time value of an option is the quantified probability that the strike price of the particular option will be in the money at expiration. The time value, if any, of an option consists of several components, called t*he Greeks* in shorthand lingo. These names, such as delta, theta, and gamma describe the various forces which affect the time value of an option. The four main factors that determine and affect the time value of an option are:

1. relationship between the strike price of the option and the current price of the underlying commodity or security,
2. time remaining until the option contract expires,
3. level of interest rates, and
4. estimated volatility of the underlying commodity or security.

Option valuation is, by itself, also the topic of hundreds of books based on pricing theory and option pricing models which calculate the time value of options. It is not within the scope of this text to discuss the extreme details of option pricing theory and option valuation. This chapter is intended to give the reader a general understanding, not a working knowledge, of options hedging, trading, and valuation. The reader should pursue other texts which cover options in more detail to learn all aspects of options before attempting to trade or invest money in them.

The relationship between the option strike price and the current price of the underlying commodity or security affects the time value of an option because the probability of an option with a strike price far above or far below the at-the-money price expiring in the money is less than if the strike price is closer to the at-the-money price. Consequently, as the price of the underlying rises, the time value of deep in-the-money calls will fall, because the probability that they will expire with intrinsic value increases to the point where the price of the calls behave much like the price of the underlying commodity or security. Similarly, as the price of the underlying falls, the time value of deep in-the-money puts will fall, because the probability that they will expire with intrinsic value increases to the point where the price of the puts behaves much like the price of the underlying commodity or security.

The time remaining, or life, until expiration of the options contract will determine and affect the time value of the option. Options with more time left until expiration, all things being equal, will have a higher time value than those with less time remaining. This is easily understood when thought of in terms of the likelihood that the price of the underlying commodity or security will move to various levels (strikes) over a longer period of time as opposed to one day, for example. For this higher probability, an option with more time remaining until expiration, all things being equal, has a higher time value than an option with a shorter life.

Interest rates play a role in the amount of time value built into an option's price. This is because the option premium is paid by the buyer to the seller at the time the option is written, and the seller can invest those funds and earn interest on them until expiration or until the option buyer exercises. Exercising is not typically done until expiration because the options retain some time value right up to their expiration, although it is less and less as the expiration date approaches. For this reason, it is more prudent for the owner of an option to sell it in the market if his or her opinion of the market has changed, rather than exercise and subsequently buy or sell the underlying before expiration. Therefore, if the level of interest rates is expected to increase, the time value of an option will likely decline, as the opportunity cost from giving up the use of funds to pay option premiums increases and option buyers are, less willing to pay in option premium. Interest rates represent a minor component of time value, except for instances where a very large premium is under consideration (i.e., the effect of a 2% annual rate of interest increase over a three month time period is not as substantial when contemplating the payment of a $5,000 option premium as opposed to a $500,000 premium).

The estimated volatility of the underlying commodity or security directly affects the time value of an option contract on it. If a commodity or security is extremely volatile, the probability is higher that an option with an out-of-the-money strike price will expire with intrinsic value (in the money). Likewise, out-of-the-money options on commodities or securities with low volatility will have less time value as the probability is lower that an out-of-the-money option will expire with intrinsic value.

Options Applications

Options can be an effective tool in hedging physical or financial positions in the natural gas market, as well as an alternative means of speculating on price direction or volatility. Because of the limited risk in buying options, many market participants will substitute an outright futures contract or futures swap transaction with an options transaction using either exchange traded standardized options or customized options traded in the OTC market.

Speculating Using Options

The use of options contracts as a speculative investment vehicle has made them somewhat notorious for their risk. This is, in part, due to the extreme degree of leverage which may be obtained through the use of options, but also due to the lack of awareness of the risks involved when writing naked options.

The leverage obtained through the use of options is similar to that of futures contracts. In the case of futures, a trader needs to put up only a small portion of the actual total value of the futures contract, or contracts, as margin when initiating a position. With options, the same concept applies, however, the trader pays only the premium for the option instead of an initial margin requirement. This is only in instances when an option is bought. When writing naked options, sellers must put up margin similar to the requirement of futures.) Therefore, a trader can control a large number of futures contracts of the underlying commodity or security by only paying the premium for the options. For example, let's suppose natural gas futures are trading $2.00 and a trader pays $0.08 for 10 of the $2.10 calls for a total cost of $8,000 (i.e., 10 x 10,000 MMBtu x $0.08 = $8,000). Let's assume at options expiration that futures are trading $2.25, and instead of exercising the calls, the trader sells them at $0.15 for total proceeds of $15,000, netting a profit of $7,000 (excluding commission) or an 87.5% return on the trade. This is a hefty return when you consider that futures prices increased only 12.5%. That's powerful leverage. Alternatively, if the trader had paid $2.00 for 10 actual futures contracts instead of the $2.10 call options on them, he would have had to put up roughly $30,000, but could have sold them at $2.25 for a $25,000 gain, or only an 83.3% return (which is still astonishing leverage). The option strategy represents only an $8,000 maximum risk of loss of capital, whereas there is no definable risk in a futures position, other than if you make the assumption that the price could go to zero (nearly impossible), which would represent a maximum capital risk of $200,000 including the initial margin requirement of $30,000. This is why many speculators trade options instead of futures.

When buying options for speculative purposes, the odds of success are theoretically against the option buyer from the beginning. That is, the price of the underlying commodity or security must rise (call options) above the option's strike price by more than the premium paid, or fall (put options) below the option's strike price by more than the premium paid, before the option is profitable at expiration. Options carry some time value prior to expiration. So, even if the break-even point, in terms of the underlying price relative to the option strike price plus (call) or minus (put) the premium, is not reached, the options could still have more value than the purchase price. A speculative option buyer is betting on a low probability occurrence (option expires in the money) in the hopes of realizing a highly leveraged return. In contrast, the writer of naked options is limiting their expected return (premium collected) and betting on the higher probability that the option will expire worthless.

Another form of speculative trading through the use of options is called *volatility trading*—a form of trading options whereby the trader is constantly hedging and re-hedging the option position in such a way that the trader's profitability on the option is not affected by the outright price level, or change in the price level, of the underlying commodity or security, but rather by the volatility, or change in volatility, of the underlying commodity or security. This is the concept, however this text will not discuss the actual methods whereby the hedges and re-hedges are done to achieve a market neutral position. This is actually called *delta hedging* to remain *delta neutral*, and is a very complicated technique which could take up an entire chapter (or book) to explain properly. Therefore, if a trader has delta hedged properly and has a long volatility position, he or she will profit if the underlying commodity or security becomes more volatile while the position is on. Volatility, however, can also decrease, which would cause a long volatility position to be unprofitable.

Hedging Fixed-Price Risk Using Options

Natural gas options provide end users and producers with a safe and sometimes affordable means (depending on volatility) with which to hedge purchases or sales, and still participate in a favorable price trend if it continues. Suppose a producer with supply at Henry Hub is concerned that natural gas prices might fall in the coming month due to warm weather. As an alternative to selling futures at the current market price ($2.15), the producer decides to pay $0.15 for the $2.15 put options (i.e., buying the $2.15 put gives the producer the right, but not the obligation, to sell futures at $2.15). At options expiration (the day before futures expiration), the $2.15 puts will either be in the money, at the money, or out of the money. Figure 4.33 shows the payout profile for the long $2.15 put position at expiration.

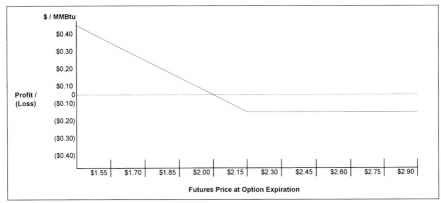

Figure 4.33. Payout Profile for Long $2.15 Put Position at $0.15 Cost

The further prices are below $2.00 (breakeven point after premium), the $2.15 puts will be worth more and more to the producer. However, if futures prices are above $2.00, the producer will lose more and more of the premium paid, but no more than the total cost of the premium.

Therefore, if futures prices at option expiration are below $2.15, the producer will exercise the put options, giving the producer a short futures position at $2.15 which it can deliver its physical supply against. However, unless futures prices at expiration are between $2.15 and $2.00, the producer would have realized a higher effective sale price had it not paid the premium for the put options. If futures prices at expiration are below $2.00, the producer would realize a higher effective sale price than had it not bought the put options. If futures prices at expiration are higher than $2.15, the producer would not exercise its right to sell at $2.15, but would instead sell its supply outright, or short futures and make delivery, at the higher prevailing cash or futures price, subtracting the premium it paid for the put options to calculate its effective sale price. If futures prices at expiration are $2.20, the producer's effective sale price would be $2.20 less the $0.15 premium for the put options, or $2.05. Again, if futures prices at option expiration are above $2.00, the producer would have realized a higher effective sales price had it not bought the put options.

End users can protect themselves from adverse price movement (higher prices) by paying premium for call options. Following a similar process as the producer, substituting call options for put options, an end user can be assured of paying no more than the call strike price, plus the premium paid, for gas supply.

Enhancing Revenues or Lowering Costs Using Options

In the natural gas market, producers are considered to be naturally long, and end users are considered to be naturally short. Due to their functions in the business activity, producers are typically sellers and end users are typically buyers. Producers are sometimes buyers if they "sell out" of their own supply, but still have additional sales opportunities, and end users are sometimes sellers if they buy too much supply for their own needs. As such, producers and end users can write covered options against these natural positions.

Suppose an end user is concerned that fixed prices at Henry Hub are going to rise in the following month due to cold weather. Because the end user knows it will have to buy physical supply at some time before the month arrives, it has a natural short position. Against this position, the end user decides to sell the $2.15 put options at $0.15, thereby collecting premium. Figure 4.34 shows the payout profile of the short $2.15 put position at expiration.

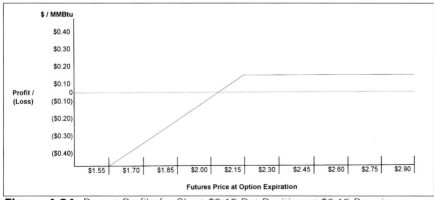

Figure 4.34. Payout Profile for Short $2.15 Put Position at $0.15 Premium Collected

The higher prices rise above $2.00 (breakeven point after premium), the more of the premium the end user will retain up to the total amount it received. On the other hand, if futures prices are below $2.15, the end user will lose more and more. However, the money the end user will lose is really only opportunity cost (forgone savings) because the end user has to buy supply sometime anyway.

If futures prices at option expiration are above $2.15, the buyer of the put options will not exercise, thereby allowing the end user to keep the full premium it received from selling the puts. The premium can then be subtracted from the cost of what the end user ultimately pays in the cash market, or futures market if taking delivery, for physical gas. However, if futures prices at expiration are between $2.15 and $2.00, the buyer of the put options would presumably exercise the puts, thereby giving the end user a long futures position at $2.15. Since the end user needed to buy supply anyway, it can take delivery of the physical gas at futures expiration. As you can see, the short sale of the put options does not guarantee a maximum price the end user has to pay, but provides it with premium, if futures prices at expiration are higher than $2.00, that it can offset its supply cost with. Alternatively, if prices at expiration are below $2.00, the short put sale obligates the end user to buy supply that it could have otherwise paid a lower price for.

Producers can generate revenue to enhance their sale prices by selling covered calls in the same way that end users can reduce their supply price by selling covered puts. In the case of a producer that has sold calls to collect premium, if futures prices at option expiration are higher than the call strike price plus the premium it received, the producer will also lose opportunity cost of being able to sell at the higher prices. Likewise, if prices fall below the strike price less the premium received, the producer is not guaranteed a minimum price for its supply, but can only apply the premium collected from the sale of calls to the price it receives after the calls expire, when calculating its effective sale price.

Swing Swap Options

A *swing swap option* is similar to ordinary options, with the exception that the underlying is neither a futures contract, nor a physical transaction, but rather the daily index price for a specific location. The concept of a swing swap option is similar to ordinary options. A swing swap put option will be profitable to the buyer of the option if the daily index price is below the strike price (either the first of the month index price or a fixed price, depending on the deal structure) beyond the premium paid for the puts. Similarly, a swing swap call option will be profitable to the buyer of the option if the daily index price is above the strike price beyond the premium paid for the calls.

The mechanics of a swing swap option, however, can be somewhat different from ordinary options. Because the underlying in a Swing swap option is the daily index price, the option can be settled (strike price versus floating price) against each day's individual index price, or the average of some or all of the daily index prices for a given month. This is an important distinction in that it can significantly alter the payout, if any, of a swing swap option. Assume a buyer pays $0.10 for a $2.00 swing swap call option on 10,000 MMBtu/d (1 contract/d) for eight days. A table of each day's daily index price follows.

Day 1	$2.00
Day 2	$2.25
Day 3	$2.50
Day 4	$2.25
Day 5	$2.00
Day 6	$1.75
Day 7	$1.50
Day 8	$1.75
Avg.	$2.00

As you can see, if the swing swap call option is settled against the average of the daily index prices, the buyer would essentially forfeit the $0.10 premium ($8,000) because the option has no intrinsic value. However, if the swing swap call option were settled against each day's individual index prices, the buyer would have realized a net profit of $7,000 (i.e., $0.15 x 10,000 MMBtu on Days 2 and 4, and $.40 x 10,000 MMBtu on Day 3). Although the method of settling swing swap options can be chosen by the buyer, the pricing is much different between settling the option against each day's price, versus the average of each day's price.

Swing swap options are used in more complex structured transactions among market participants.

In summary, options are another of the many different tools which are used in the natural gas market to take or hedge risk. If used properly, and if the potential risks of capital are fully understood, options can be a valuable asset to any trader, producer, or end user.

Summary of Hedging and Trading Instruments. There are several financial and physical tools available in the natural gas market that can help market participants hedge risk, facilitate customer requests, speculate, or enhance revenues and reduce costs. Through the use of these hedging and trading instruments, natural gas trading can be much more than buying or selling gas at fixed prices. In fact, there are possibly hundreds of different combinations of transactions which can help traders, producers, and end users accomplish many objectives. Of course, the ultimate goal is to generate profits. What these hedging and trading instruments do for the natural gas market is allow for market participants to pursue their own methods of generating profits, either through managing risk or leveraging it.

Chapter 5

Structured Transactions

This part of the book covers the procedures and tools used to hedge more complex natural gas transactions with consumers and suppliers and transactions which are not necessarily between a trader and a customer. It is assumed that readers of this part of the text have a thorough understanding of natural gas market terminology, the hedging and trading instruments covered in Part IV, and the business activities in the market.

Buying High and Selling Low for a Profit

At first glance, buying high and selling low for a profit seems like an impossible task. However, with basis swaps and futures or fixed-for-floating swaps, a trader can profit by buying gas at a high fixed price and selling it at a lower fixed price. In fact, this is one of the best strategies for trading natural gas. It is often easier to sell gas at fixed prices when the market is trading at a relatively low level and buy gas at fixed prices when the market is trading at a relatively high level.

Suppose futures prices have been trading at $2.00, but suddenly break out to the upside and trade up to $2.25. Using the Permian basin as an example, let's assume prices there have risen from $1.75 to $1.95 during the same upside price break out. A trader knows a producer that likes to sell its supply at a fixed price instead of index, so he calls the producer and bids $1.95 for the producer's Permian supply. Because of the recent price increase, the producer decides to sell to the trader at $1.95. To hedge the fixed-price risk, the trader immediately sells futures at $2.25, thereby converting the fixed price into a minus $0.30 differential to futures, a differential the trader feels is at the low, or wide end of its recent trading range.

The following week, futures prices fall back to $2.00 and Permian prices again fall back to $1.75. Now, the trader calls an end user he knows that likes to buy gas at fixed prices, and offers to sell Permian at $1.75. Because the end user thinks Permian prices will probably go back up to the $1.95 level, it agrees to pay $1.75 to the trader for the gas. Again, to hedge the fixed-price risk and unwind its current long differential position, the trader immediately pays $2.00 for futures, thereby converting the fixed sale price into a minus $0.25 differential to futures, which closes out the minus $0.30 long position. The trade is done and the trader has made a $0.05 margin. Figure 5.1 illustrates

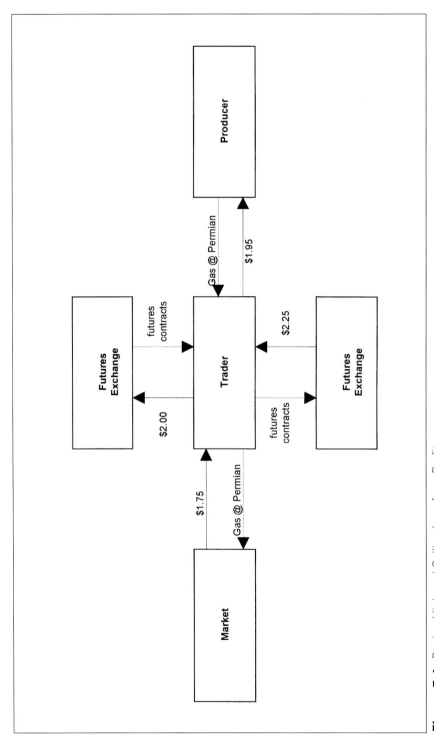

Figure 5.1. Buying High and Selling Low for a Profit

the mechanics of the transactions, and a schedule of payments and receipts follows to show the trader's total profit.

Pay to producer (−)	$1.95
Futures sold (+)	$2.25
Receive from end-user (+)	$1.75
Futures bought (−)	$2.00
Profit /loss on trade	$0.05 x number of contracts

The trader converted the fixed price risk into less-volatile basis risk and was successful at selling the gas at a tighter differential than the purchase. However, if the basis market had widened between the time the trader bought the gas and the time it was sold, the trader would have been at risk of losing money. To hedge against any adverse movement in basis, natural gas traders will typically use basis swaps to hedge that risk, thereby converting the basis differential to futures into an index related price because it is less volatile, as they wait for the right time to close the physical position.

In this example, after paying $1.95 for the Permian supply, and selling futures at $2.25 to lock in the minus $0.30 differential, the trader could have sold a Permian basis swap at L3D minus $0.30 or tighter to effectively eliminate the basis risk and convert the purchase price into index. Then, when the trader had an opportunity to sell the supply at a fixed price (either higher or lower than the original fixed price paid for the supply), he should sell the supply at a tighter differential than he can buy a basis swap to unwind the trade with. Here's an example.

Pay to producer (−)	$1.95
Futures sold (+)	$2.25
Receive from basis swap #1 (+)	L3D − $0.29
Pay to basis swap #1 (−)	Index
Receive from end-user (+)	$1.75
Futures bought (−)	$2.00
Pay to basis swap #2 (−)	L3D − $0.26
Receive from basis swap #2 (+)	Index
Profit /loss on trade	$0.02 x number of contracts

The profit potential is lessened as the risk is reduced from basis risk to index risk. However, basis in some regions of the country is sometimes more volatile than fixed prices, so if a trader has basis risk in these regions, a basis hedge to get back to index is usually the position to hold.

Hedging Firm Transportation

Traders are often presented with opportunities to purchase released firm transportation capacity from either a pipeline or a third party. What is the best way to determine a fair price for the capacity and what is the best way to hedge against the loss in value of the capacity if it is purchased? The difference in the value of the basis swaps for the two locations in question (i.e., receipt point and delivery point of the transportation capacity) will determine a fair price for the capacity, and by buying the basis swap which corresponds to the receipt point location of the capacity and selling the basis swap which corresponds to the delivery point location of the capacity, the value (spread) can be locked-in if the trader should buy the capacity at that price (spread) or lower.

For example, let's suppose a trader has an opportunity to buy firm transportation capacity on NGPL from Oklahoma to Chicago city-gate (c.g.) for the month of June. If NGPL Mid-continent basis swaps are trading L3D minus $0.20, and Chicago c.g. basis swaps are trading L3D plus $0.10 for June, the fair value for firm transportation capacity from NGPL Mid-continent to Chicago c.g. for June should be $0.30, inclusive of demand charges and fuel.

Assuming the trader then pays $0.30 for the firm capacity, what risk does the trader have? Essentially, the trader is exposed to Chicago c.g. prices going lower in June relative to NGPL M.C. and/or NGPL M.C. prices going higher in June relative to Chicago c.g. prices. This represents basis risk between Chicago c.g. and NGPL M.C. The trader is exposed to the June NGPL M.C. basis to Chicago c.g. tightening, rendering the transportation capacity less valuable. The hedge therefore is to protect the trader from this happening. This can be done by simultaneously buying the June NGPL M.C. basis swap, and selling the June Chicago c.g. basis swap and locking-in enough of a spread from the difference to offset the cost of the firm transportation. In addition, the trader must pay June NGPL M.C. index or lower for physical gas on NGPL in Oklahoma and sell physical gas at Chicago c.g. at the June Chicago c.g. index or higher. Figure 5.2 illustrates the mechanics of this transaction, assuming the trader paid L3D minus $0.20 for an NGPL M.C. basis swap, sold a Chicago c.g. basis swap at L3D plus $0.10, and paid NGPL M.C. index for gas at the receipt point and sold gas at Chicago c.g. index plus $0.02 at the delivery point.

Pay to transportation (−)	$0.30
Receive from Chicago basis swap (+)	L3D + $0.10
Pay to Chicago basis swap (−)	Chicago index
Receive from Chicago market (+)	Chicago index + $0.02
Pay to NGPL M.C. basis swap (−)	L3D − $0.20
Receive from NGPL M.C. basis swap (+)	NGPL M.C. index
Pay to NGPL M.C. supply (−)	NGPL M.C. index
Profit /loss on trade	$0.02 x number of contracts

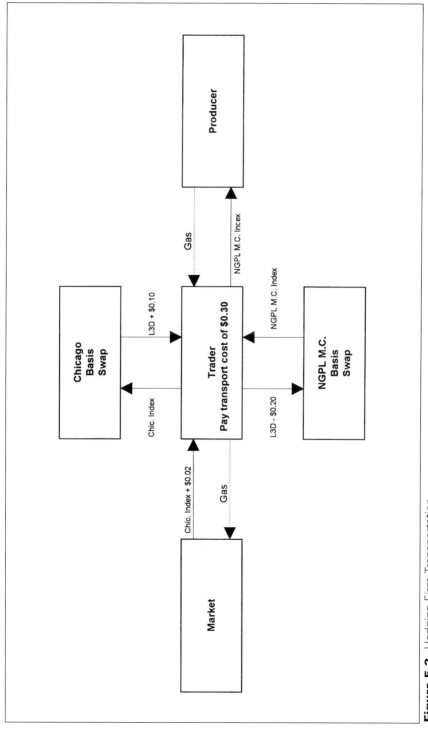

Figure 5.2. Hedging Firm Transportation

The trade is completely hedged, regardless of the difference between NGPL M.C. and Chicago c.g. indexes.

With regard to determining fair value for firm transportation by evaluating the difference between the production area basis swap (NGPL M.C. in this example) and the market area basis swap (Chicago c.g.), if transport is actually for sale (released) at a price which is less than the difference between the basis swaps, transportation arbitrageurs will bid up the cost of capacity as they try to buy that capacity and hedge it for a locked-in profit. Likewise, if transportation is valued above the difference between the basis swaps, either transportation arbitrageurs will offer synthetic firm transportation at lower prices as they attempt to short the capacity and hedge it, or the pipelines or firm shippers will be stuck with excess capacity, requiring them to discount until the cost of capacity becomes more fairly valued in terms of the difference between the production area basis swaps and the market area basis swaps.

Transportation arbitrageurs can synthetically sell short firm transportation capacity by doing a physical swap with another party, whereby the arbitrageur pays an index price for the physical supply in the production area and sells physical supply in the market area to that same party at the same index price plus the premium between the two basis swaps. This is also known as artificial transportation capacity.

If transportation capacity from NGPL M.C. to Chicago c.g. is $0.32 bid by another trader, and an arbitrageur can pay L3D plus $0.10 for a Chicago c.g. basis swap and sell an NGPL M.C. basis swap at L3D minus $0.20, thereby paying $0.30 net, the arbitrageur can potentially capture a $0.02 / MMBtu profit. This is done by entering into a physical exchange with the customer wherein the customer agrees to sell gas at NGPL M.C. to the arbitrageur at NGPL M.C. index flat and in return pay NGPL M.C. index plus $0.32 for the same gas delivered at Chicago c.g. To hedge his basis risk between the two points, the arbitrageur first pays L3D plus $0.10 for the Chicago c.g. basis swap, then sells the NGPL M.C. basis swap at L3D minus $0.20. Then, to hedge the physical delivery risk, the arbitrageur sells the physical supply on NGPL M.C. at NGPL M.C. index flat or higher, and pays Chicago c.g. index for gas at the delivery point in Chicago. Figure 5.3 illustrates the mechanics of this transaction.

Pay to Chicago supply (−)	Chicago index
Receive from Chicago basis swap (+)	Chicago index
Pay to Chicago basis swap (−)	L3D + $0.10
Receive from NGPL M.C. basis swap (+)	L3D − $0.20
Pay to NGPL M.C. basis swap (−)	NGPL M.C. index
Receive from NGPL M.C. market (+)	NGPL M.C. index
Pay for physical to third party (−)	NGPL M.C. index
Receive for physical from third party (+)	NGPL M.C. index + $0.32
Profit /loss on trade	$0.02 x number of contracts

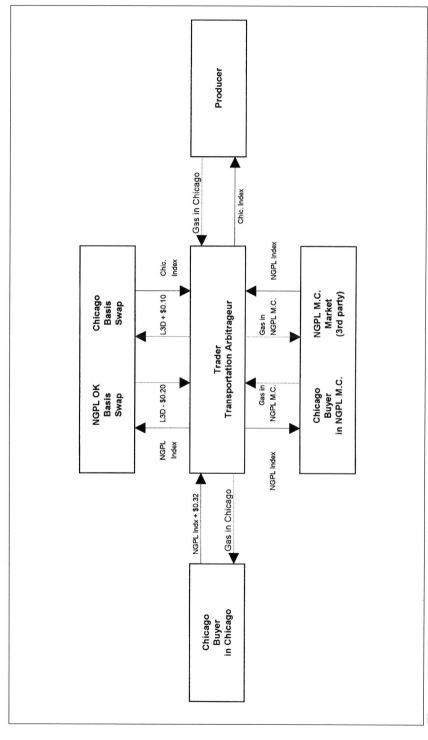

Figure 5.3. Firm Transportation Arbitrage

Therefore, as a result of the existence of a basis swap market at each location corresponding to the receipt and delivery points of various transportation legs, firm transportation capacity can be more accurately evaluated as well as hedged in those instances where the future value of the capacity is in question.

Selling Physical Swing Options to Producers

A common transaction between a producer and a buyer is one in which the buyer grants the producer the right to increase the amount of gas it is selling to the buyer at the original price in the transaction, with advanced notice, during a given month. Due to changes in demand during the month, producers often have more gas available during periods of low demand (e.g. weekends) and like to structure a transaction which enables them to flex-up on the amount of gas they are selling to a buyer at a predetermined price during these times. Here is an example where a producer is selling 10,000 MMBtu/d (one contract/d) to a trader at a fixed price, and has the right to increase the volume by 10,000 MMBtu/d during the month at that price with two day's advanced notice to allow for the nomination change.

There are two risks which must be managed by traders in a transaction such as this. First, they must have a physical market for the supply if the producer does decide to exercise its right to increase the amount of gas it is selling (assuming the trader does not have access to a storage facility). Since the trader does not know when the producer will exercise this option during the month, they must have a physical short position in the day-to-day market throughout the entire month to have a home for the gas if and when the producer exercises its swing option right. The additional sale can either be made to the same market that is buying the original volume, or it can be made to a different market. So, in our example above, because the traders are buying one contract/d from the producer and granting the producer the right to flex up to two contracts/d, they need to sell two contracts/d for the entire month to a market (or markets), half of which will be covered by the original volume from the producer, the other half of which will be covered with supply in the day-to-day market until (if ever) the producer exercises its right to increase the volume in the original sale.

The second risk which must be managed is the price risk. More specifically, traders must hedge against daily prices during the month trading lower than the fixed price they are paying to the producer. In addition, to hedge the physical short position which will be covered with supply from the day-to-day market, the traders must hedge against daily prices during the month trading higher than the fixed price they have physically sold short. To hedge against falling prices during the month, traders need to buy a swing swap put option (pay premium, receive difference between first-of-month index and daily index when daily index is less than first-of-month index), and, to hedge the physical short position against rising prices during the month, traders need to buy a swing swap (pay first of the month index, receive daily index). It is assumed that the producer will only exercise its right to increase the volume it is selling to the trader during the month if prices in the day-to-day market are below the predetermined fixed price it is receiving from the trader. In other words, the producer will only exercise if the option has intrinsic value. Thus, if prices rise during the month, and traders are buying gas in the day-to-day market at higher prices than the fixed-price they are short at, the profit from the swing swap will offset the physical losses and keep the traders position hedged. Likewise, if prices fall during the month and the producer increases the volume it is selling, the gain from the swing swap put option will offset the loss on the swing swap and the traders will substitute the increased volume from the producer for supply they had been buying in the day-to-day market.

Below are the steps which traders must take to hedge the physical risk in the trade, assuming they are buying one contract/d from the producer, with the producer having the right to increase the volume to two contracts/d during the month.

1. Sell two contracts/d for entire month
2. Buy one contract/d for the entire month, and buy one contract/d each day in the day-to-day market
3. Substitute day-to-day swing supply with increase in supply from producer if exercised.

This will effectively make the traders short one contract/d from day-to-day during the month which they can supply with gas in the day-to-day market until (if ever) the producer exercises its right to put the additional one contract/d.

Before discussing the details of what fixed price the trader will be able to pay the producer, and how the trader will hedge the price risk between the day-to-day price and that fixed price, let's assume that the trader is selling two contracts/d to one buyer at the first of the month index plus $0.02, and that the trader can pay exactly the daily index for gas in the day-to-day market. Furthermore, to hedge this part of the price risk, we will assume the trader buys a swing swap wherein the trader pays the first-of-month index price and receives the daily index price. Although the final payment or receipt in the swing swap (not the swing swap option) is based on the average of the daily indexes, we are going to be looking at this transaction from a day-to-day perspective. Furthermore, we will assume the producer can only flex up by one contract/d or nothing at all, although the volume could be between zero and one contract/d and the hedge will still work.

So how does the trader arrive at the fixed price that can be paid to the producer? It depends on two variables—the fixed price the trader can receive for a fixed-float Index swap (to hedge the risk between the index price and the fixed price) and the premium the trader pays for the swing swap put option. Generally speaking, the trader can pay the producer the strike price of the swing swap put option. However, for the transaction to work properly (profitably), the trader must be able to sell a fixed-float index swap at a fixed price which is above the price paid to the producer by the amount of the premium for the swing swap option with a strike price equal to the price to the producer.

For example, if trader can sell Index swap at $2.25, trader can pay producer $2.20 if trader can pay $0.05 for $2.20 swing swap put option and $2.15 if trader can pay $0.10 for $2.15 swing swap put option.

Therefore, fixed price to producer equals fixed-float index swap bid less premium cost (offer) for swing swap put option at the respective strike price. Because of this relationship, the fixed price the trader can pay the producer will always be out of the money. There is no such thing as a free option.

For this example, assume that the trader can sell a fixed-float index swap at $2.10 (one contract/d), and can pay $0.10 for the $2.00 swing swap put option (one contract/d). As a result, the trader can pay the producer a $2.00 fixed price for one contract/d of physical gas and allow the producer to increase the volume by one contract/d at $2.00 with two day's notice at any time during the month or for the entire month. Figure 5.4 illustrates how the final transaction would look.

This is a schedule of payments and receipts which shows the net outcome of a specific day where that day's price is $2.25 (producer does not exercise).

Pay to producer (−)	$2.00	(1 contract/d)
Receive from fixed-float index swap (+)	$2.10	
Pay to fixed-float index swap (−)	Index	
Receive from market (+)	Index + $0.02	(1 contract/d)
Profit on first contract	$0.12 x 1 contract = $1,200	
Receive from market (+)	Index + $0.02	(1 contract/d)
Pay to swing swap (−)	Index	
Receive from swing swap (+)	$2.25	
Pay to day-to-day supplier (−)	$2.25	(1 contract/d)
Pay to swing swap put option (−)	$0.10	
Receive from swing swap put option (+)	$0.00	put has no intrinsic value)
Loss on second contract	($0.08) x 1 contract = ($800)	
Total profit	$1,200 − $800 = $400 for the day	

Here is a schedule of payments and receipts which shows the net outcome of a specific day where that day's price is $1.75 (producer exercises).

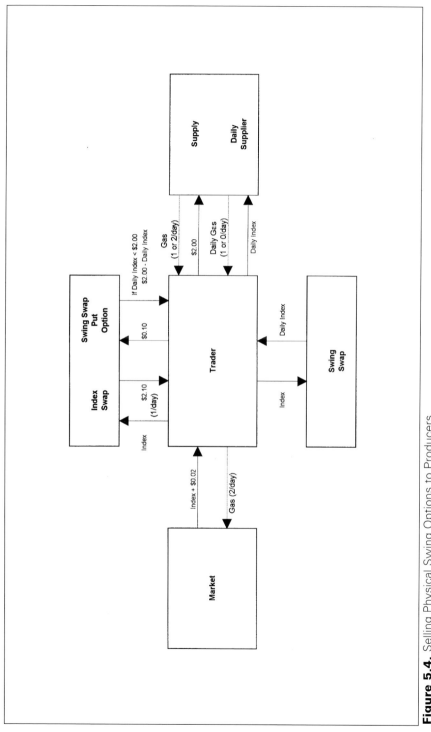

Figure 5.4. Selling Physical Swing Options to Producers

Pay to producer (−)	$2.00	(1 contract/d)
Receive from fixed-float index swap (+)	$2.10	
Pay to fixed-float index swap (−)	Index	
Receive from market (+)	Index + $0.02 (1 contract/d)	
Profit on first contract	$0.12 * 1 contract = $1,200	
Receive from market (+)	Index + $0.02 (1 contract/d)	
Pay to swing swap (−)	Index	
Receive from swing swap (+)	$1.75	
Pay to producer (−)	$2.00	(1 contract/d)
Pay to day-to-day supplier (−)	$0.00	(no supply needed)
Pay to swing swap put option (−)	$0.10	
Receive from swing swap put option (+)	$0.25	($2.00 - $1.75 = $0.25)
Loss on second contract	($0.08) x 1 contract = ($800)	
Total profit	$1,200 − $800 = $400 for the day	

Although this is a fairly complex transaction, it should be clear that this type of deal structure can be provided to a seller and be hedged as in the example above to eliminate both the physical risk as well as the intra-month price risk. Note that the profit on the trade is most easily determined by the premium over index the sale is made to the market. Sellers often like to enter into trades that are below market, however if the seller foresees a rough month ahead in terms of fluctuations in demand, swing swap options can provide a trader with an alternative deal structure to meet the needs of the seller.

Selling Physical Swing Options to End Users

A common transaction between an end user and a seller is one in which the seller grants the end user (buyer) the right to increase the amount of gas it is buying from the seller at the original price in the transaction, with advanced notice, during a given month. These types of transactions are common because, due to changes in demand during the month, end users often need more gas supply during periods of high demand and like to structure a transaction which enables them to flex-up on the amount of gas they are buying from a seller at a predetermined fixed price during these times. Here is an example where an end user is paying a fixed price for 10,000 MMBtu/d (one contract/d) to a trader, and has the right to increase the volume by 10,000 MMBtu/d during the month at that price with two day's advanced notice (to allow for the nomination change).

There are two risks faced by traders which must be managed in a transaction such as this. First, they must have physical supply available if the end user decides to exercise its right to increase the amount of gas it is buying (assuming the traders do not have access to a storage facility). Therefore, since the traders do not know when the end user will exercise during the month, they must have a physical *long* position in the day-to-day market throughout the entire month to be able to have gas supply when (if ever) the end-user exercises its swing option right. The additional supply can either be bought from the same supplier which is selling the original volume to the trader, or it can be bought from a different supplier. So, because the traders are selling one contract/d to the end user and granting the end user the right to flex-up to two contracts/d, they need to buy two contracts/d for the entire month from a supplier (or suppliers), half of which will be sold as the original sale to the end user, the other half of which will be sold to a buyer in the day-to-day market until (if ever) the end-user exercises its swing option right.

The second risk which must be managed is the price risk. More specifically, traders must hedge against daily prices during the month trading higher than the fixed price they are receiving from the end user. In addition, to hedge the physical long position which will be sold to a buyer in the day-to-day market, the traders must hedge against daily prices during the month trading lower than the fixed price they have bought long for. To hedge against rising prices during the month, the traders need to buy a swing swap call option (pay premium, receive difference between first-of-month index and daily index when daily index is greater than first-of-month index). To hedge the physical long position against falling prices during the month, the traders need to sell a swing swap (receive first of the month index, pay daily index). It is assumed that the end user will only exercise its right to increase the volume it is buying from the trader during the month if prices in the day-to-day market are above the predetermined fixed price it is paying to the trader. Thus, if prices fall during the month, and the traders are selling gas in the day-to-day market at lower prices than the fixed-price they are long from, the profit from the swing swap will offset the physical losses and keep the traders position hedged. Likewise, if prices rise during the month and the end user increases the volume it is buying from the traders, the gain from the swing swap call option will offset the loss on the swing swap and the traders will substitute the increased volume taken by the end user for the buyer they had been selling to in the day-to-day market.

Here are the steps which the traders must take to hedge the physical risk in the trade, assuming they are selling one contract/d to the end user, allowing the end user the right to increase the volume to two contracts/d during the month.

1. Buy two contracts/d for entire month,

2. Sell one contract/d for the entire month, and sell one contract/d each day in the day-to-day market, and

3. Substitute day-to-day sale with increase in sales volume to end user if exercised.

This will effectively make the traders long one contract/d for the entire month which they can sell in the day-to-day market until (if ever) the end user exercises its right to call on the additional one contract/d from the trader.

Before discussing the details of the fixed price the traders should sell to the end user for, and how the traders will hedge the price risk between the day-to-day price and that fixed price, let's assume that the traders are paying the first of the month index minus $0.02 for two contracts/d from one seller, and that the traders can sell gas at exactly the daily index for a given day in the day-to-day market. Furthermore, to hedge this part of the price risk, we will assume the traders buy a swing swap wherein the traders pay the first-of-month index and receive the daily index. Although the final payment or receipt in the swing swap is based on the average of the daily indexes, we are going to be looking at this transaction from a day-to-day perspective. Furthermore, we will assume the end user can only flex-up by one contract/d or nothing at all, although the volume could be between zero and one contract/d and the hedge will still work.

So how the traders arrive at the fixed price that they should receive from the end user? It depends on two variables—the fixed price the traders must pay for a fixed-float index swap (to hedge the risk between the Index price and the fixed price), and the premium the traders pay for the swing swap call option. Generally speaking, the trader can sell to the end user at the strike price of the swing swap call option. However, for the transaction to work properly, the trader must be able to pay a fixed price for an index swap which is below the price received from the end user by the amount of the premium paid for the swing swap option, with a strike price equal to the price received from the end user.

For example, if traders can pay $2.15 for an index swap, traders should sell to end user at: $2.20 if traders can pay $0.05 for $2.20 swing swap call option, or $2.25 if traders can pay $0.10 for $2.25 swing swap call option. Therefore, fixed price from end user equals fixed-float index swap cost (offer) plus premium offer for call option at the respective strike price

Because of this relationship, the fixed price the trader sells to the end user for will always be out of the money. There is no such thing as a free option.

For this example, we will assume that the trader can pay $2.10 for a fixed-float index swap (one contract/d), and can pay $0.10 for the $2.20 swing swap call option (one contract/d). As a result, the trader can sell one contract/d of physical gas to the end user at $2.20and allow the end user to increase the volume by one contract/d at $2.20 with two day's notice at any time during the month or for the entire month. Figure 5.5 illustrates how the final transaction would look:

Here is a schedule of payments and receipts which shows the net outcome of a specific day where that day's price is $2.10 (end user does not exercise).

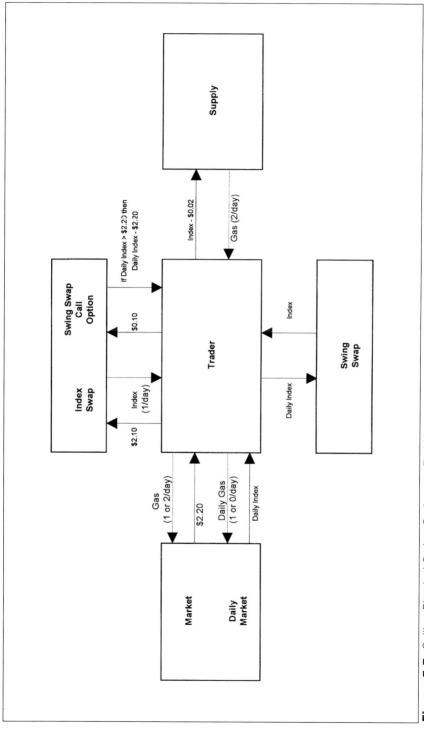

Figure 5.5. Selling Physical Swing Options to End-Users

Receive from end user (+)	$2.20	(1 contract/d)
Pay to fixed-float index swap (−)	$2.10	
Receive from fixed-float index swap (+)	Index	
Pay to supplier (−)	Index − $0.02 (1 contract/d)	

Profit on first contract	$0.12 x 1 contract = $1,200

Pay to supplier (−)	Index − $0.02 (1 contract/d)	
Receive from swing swap (+)	Index	
Pay to swing swap (−)	$2.10	
Receive from day-to-day market (+)	$2.10	(1 contract/d)
Pay to swing swap call option (−)	$0.10	
Receive from swing swap call option (+)	$0.00	(call has no intrinsic value)

Loss on second contract	($0.08) x 1 contract = ($800)

Total profit	$1,200 − $800 = $400 for the day

Next is a schedule of payments and receipts which shows the net outcome of a specific day where that day's index price is $2.30 (end user exercises).

Receive from end user (+)	$2.20	(1 contract/d)
Pay to fixed-float index swap (-)	$2.10	
Receive from fixed-float index swap (+)	Index	
Pay to supplier (−)	Index − $0.02 (1 contract/d)	

Profit on first contract	$0.12 x 1 contract = $1,200

Pay to supplier (−)	Index − $0.02 (1 contract/d)	
Receive from swing swap (+)	Index	
Pay to swing swap (−)	$2.30	
Receive from day-to-day market (+)	$0.00	(no sale necessary)
Receive from end-user (+)	$2.20	
Pay to swing swap call option (−)	$0.10	
Receive from swing swap call option (+)	$0.10 ($2.30 − $2.20 = $0.10)	

Loss on second contract	($0.08) x 1 contract = ($800)

Total profit	$1,200 − $800 = $400 for the day

One major point needs to be made with regard to this example. The assumption that the trader can pay index minus $0.02 for gas supply is not very realistic in the real world market. Although it is possible in some regions, buying physical gas at a discount to index is nearly impossible at the majority of trading locations. The discount the trader was able to buy gas for in the above example represents the total profit margin on the trade. However, if the trader had to pay index flat, or even a premium over index for the supply, the trade would break even or lose. Consequently, if a trader cannot pay a discount to index, the trader's profit margin should be built in somewhere else in the transaction. Since there are two possible outcomes in a trade such as this (trade is exercised or not exercised), the trader should be sure to include a profit margin which would be reflected in either outcome. For example, the trader could sell gas to the end user at a price which is higher than the strike price of the swing swap call option. This alteration however, would only result in a profit for the trader on those days when the end user exercises its physical swing option right. So, in addition to this alteration, the trader could also attempt to sell gas in the day-to-day market at a price higher than the daily index price, but this is usually a difficult task, similar to paying a discount to index for supply. Another alternative would be for the trader to try and negotiate a higher price received from the sale of the swing swap itself, such as paying the daily index price, but receiving the first of the month index price plus $0.02, for example. Consequently, although this is a more complex transaction than selling a physical swing option to a producer, it should be clear that this type of deal structure can be provided to a buyer and be hedged to eliminate both the physical risk as well as the intra-month price risk. Buyers often like to enter into trades that are above market, however if the buyer foresees a rough month ahead in terms of fluctuations in demand, swing swap options can provide a trader with an alternative deal structure to meet the needs of the buyer.

Trading Physical Gas in One Location Priced at Index for Another Location

This type of structured transaction is not really that common, but can sometimes be appealing to either a buyer or a seller. The concept is to simply enter into a transaction at a specific location and price the gas based on the index price for another location. This is essentially a basis trade between the two different locations. Such transactions might appeal to a buyer who thinks the index price at the remote location will be lower than the price at the physical delivery point or to a seller that thinks the index price at the remote location will be higher than the price at the physical delivery point. One important detail regarding such a trade is that at the time the transaction is proposed, the prices at the two locations must be considered equal. If the two prices are not equal, an adjustment must be made at the time the trade is negotiated. For example, if prices in the Permian basin are trading $1.75, but prices in the

San Juan basin are trading $1.50, representing a difference in price of $0.25, a physical trade in the Permian basin priced using the San Juan Index should command a $0.25 premium. Likewise, a physical trade in the San Juan basin priced using the Permian index should command a $0.25 discount. The example below will help clarify the mechanics of such a transaction.

Let's suppose a trader has an opportunity to pay a Houston Ship Channel(HSC) index price to a producer for gas delivered in the Permian basin for the month of June. What premium or discount to the HSC index should the trader bid for the gas? By looking at the basis swaps for each region, the trader can determine the relative prices, and therefore conclude if he should pay a discount or a premium to the HSC index for gas delivered in the Permian. Here is an example.

EPNG Permian		HSC	
Bid	**Offer**	**Bid**	**Offer**
- $0.25	- $0.23	-$0.10	- $0.08
Mid-mkt.		**Mid-mkt.**	
- $0.24		- $0.09	

From these quotes, the trader can calculate that for the month of June, the market currently values Permian gas at a $0.15 discount to gas at HSC. Because he or she is looking at the difference between the mid-markets of each market for the basis swaps, the trader knows this is an approximate value. Let's assume the trader is a good negotiator and is able to pay HSC index minus $0.17 to the producer for the gas in Permian. Furthermore, we will also assume the trader is selling the gas in the Permian at Permian index. Figure 5.6a illustrates this transaction and the risk that the trader is exposed to up to this point.

As you can see, the trader has risk between HSC index minus $0.17 and Permian index. The trader has essentially sold a Permian basin to Houston Ship Channel spread at $0.17. That is, if the spread is greater than $0.17, the trader will lose money. If the spread is less than $0.17, the trader will make money. To hedge this risk, therefore, the trader needs to buy an HSC to Permian spread and effectively lock-in less than a $0.17 spread to make a profit. This is done through the use of basis swaps. In order to buy the spread, the trader will need to buy an HSC basis swap (i.e., pay differential, receive index), and simultaneously sell a Permian basis swap (i.e., receive differential, pay index), thereby paying out the difference between the values of the two basis swaps. Let's assume the trader is able to pay L3D minus $0.09 for the HSC basis swap, and the trader is able to sell the Permian basis swap at L3D minus $0.24, resulting in a spread of only $0.15. Although it is not paid up front, payment or receipt between the two swaps is determined separately as it is in normal basis swap transactions. Assuming the two basis swaps are transacted with different parties, the next diagram illustrates the completed transaction,

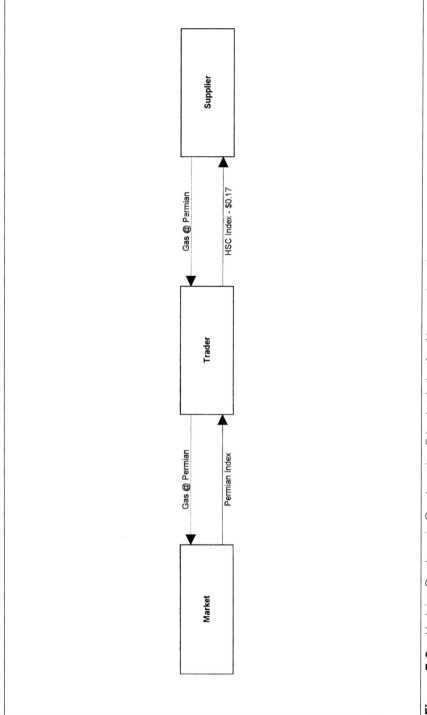

Figure 5.6a. Hedging Purchase in One Location Priced at Index for Alternate Location

and the schedule of payments and receipts which follows shows the trader's net profit.

Pay to supplier in Permian (−)	HSC index − $0.17
Receive from HSC basis swap (+)	HSC index
Pay to HSC basis swap (−)	L3D − $0.09
Receive from Permian basis swap (+)	L3D − $0.24
Pay to Permian basis swap (−)	Permian index
Receive from market in Permian (+)	Permian index
Total profit	$0.02 x number of contracts

Spreads can be bought and sold as a package with one counterparty. The payment, if any, and or the receipt, if any, is based on the difference between the two indices and the negotiated spread. Below is what the schedule of payments and receipts would look like if the trader in the example had paid $0.15 for the HSC to Permian spread to one counterparty instead of doing each leg of the spread separately with two different counterparties:

Pay to supplier in Permian (−)	HSC index − $0.17
Receive from market in Permian (+)	Permian index
Receive from HSC / Permian spread (+)	HSC Index − Permian index
Pay to HSC / Permian spread (−)	$0.15
Total profit	$0.02 x number of contracts

An easier way of looking at the schedule would be to treat the physical purchase and sale as a spread itself (i.e., paying the higher priced index for gas, selling at the lower priced index, receiving the spread).

Pay to physical spread (−)	HSC Index − Permian Index
Receive from physical spread (+)	$0.17
Pay to HSC / Permian spread (−)	$0.15
Receive from HSC / Permian spread (+)	HSC Index − Permian index
Total profit	$0.02 x number of contracts

These types of transactions might appeal to those customers interested in taking on basis spread risk in the hopes of improving their ultimate effective price on a transaction. However, more savvy customers would probably not enter into a physical transaction such as this, but would instead enter into a basis spread on their own, thus saving the profit made by the third-party trader. Nonetheless, this can be an alternate pricing method used to meet the needs of customers wishing to price their transactions at indexes for other locations.

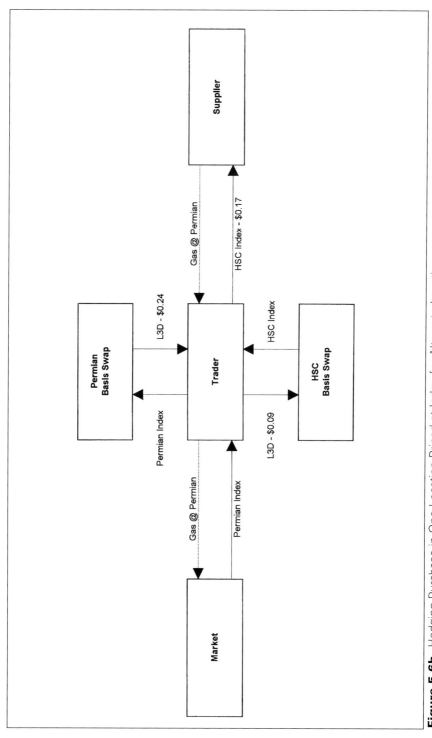

Figure 5.6b. Hedging Purchase in One Location Priced at Index for Alternate Location

Buying Index Gas
with a Floor from a Seller

Natural gas sellers which are primarily concerned with the outright fixed price level received for their gas supply may have interest in selling gas at an index related price with a predetermined fixed-price floor (minimum price). This pricing method can be provided by a trader to a seller through the use of index put options. Index options are similar to options on futures, with the exception that they are struck against the index for a particular location. By embedding an index put into a transaction, a trader can buy from a seller at an index related price, guarantee the seller a minimum fixed price, and protect itself from prices falling below that level.

Suppose a seller would like to sell Permian gas to a trader at an index related price with a floor for the following month. How much of a discount to index should the trader pay to the seller for the gas and what floor price can the trader give the seller? It depends on the premium the trader will have to pay for an index put, as well as the profit margin the trader wants to earn. We will assume the trader can earn a profit if it pays an effective price of index flat for the gas. The floor price the seller receives will be below the current market price for Permian gas for the following month.) For example, if Permian gas is worth $2.15, and the Permian $2.05 index put is offered at $0.05, the trader should bid the seller index minus $0.05 for Permian gas with a $2.00 floor. Why can't the trader give the seller a $2.05 floor instead of a $2.00 floor? Because the trader must be able to recoup the premium paid for the option. Here are some sample outcomes which will help clarify the trader's effective purchase price.

Index	Index - $0.05	Seller's Floor	Seller's Price	Index Strike	Option Premium	Trader's Price
$2.15	$2.10	$2.00	$2.10	$2.05	$0.05	$2.15
$2.10	$2.05	$2.00	$2.05	$2.05	$0.05	$2.10
$2.05	$2.00	$2.00	$2.00	$2.05	$0.05	$2.05
$2.00	$1.95	$2.00	$2.00	$2.05	$0.05	$2.00
$1.95	$1.90	$2.00	$2.00	$2.05	$0.05	$1.95
$1.90	$1.85	$2.00	$2.00	$2.05	$0.05	$1.90

The trader's effective purchase price is always equal to the index. When index is less than the index strike price, the trader's purchase price is calculated as the seller's price plus the option premium minus the index strike-index. When index is greater than the index strike price, the trader's purchase price is the seller's price plus the option premium.

The difficult part of a transaction such as this is finding a seller willing to sell at a discount to index in order to receive downside price protection. As many of the sales representatives at major producing companies are rated based on how high a premium over index they are able to sell the company's production, this form of structured pricing strategy probably won't entice them to proceed with this type transaction. However, if a trading company had speculatively paid $1.90 for Permian gas, and the market subsequently rallied to $2.15, as in the previous example, it might be willing to enter into a sale at a discount to index, still locking in a $2.00 floor for (a $0.10 minimum profit on the trade), allowing for more profit if the market price continues to increase.

Selling Index Gas with a Cap to a Buyer

Natural gas buyers which are primarily concerned with the outright fixed price level paid for their gas supply may have interest in paying an index related price with a predetermined fixed-price cap. This pricing method can be provided by a trader to a buyer through the use of index call options. By embedding an index call into a transaction, a trader can sell to a buyer at an index related price, guarantee the buyer a maximum fixed price, and protect itself from prices rising above that level.

Suppose a buyer would like to pay a trader an index related price with a cap for Permian gas for the following month. How much of a premium to Index should the trader sell the gas to the buyer for, and what cap price can the trader give the buyer? It depends on the premium the trader will have to pay for an index call, as well as the profit margin the trader wants to earn. We will assume the trader can earn a profit if the gas sells at an effective price of index plus $0.02. The cap price the buyer pays will be above the current market price for Permian gas for the following month. For example, if Permian gas is worth $2.15, and the Permian $2.23 index call is offered at $0.05, the trader would offer the buyer Permian gas at index plus $0.07 with a $2.30 cap. Here are some sample outcomes which will help clarify the trader's effective sale price.

Index	Index + $0.07	Buyer's Cap	Buyer's Price	Index Strike	Option Premium	Trader's Price
$2.40	$2.47	$2.30	$2.30	$2.23	$0.05	$2.42
$2.35	$2.42	$2.30	$2.30	$2.23	$0.05	$2.37
$2.30	$2.37	$2.30	$2.30	$2.23	$0.05	$2.32
$2.25	$2.32	$2.30	$2.30	$2.23	$0.05	$2.27
$2.20	$2.27	$2.30	$2.27	$2.23	$0.05	$2.22
$2.15	$2.22	$2.30	$2.22	$2.23	$0.05	$2.17
$2.10	$2.17	$2.30	$2.17	$2.23	$0.05	$2.12

The trader's effective sale price is always equal to index plus $0.02. When index is greater than the index strike price, the trader's sale price is calculated as buyer's price minus the option premium plus index minus index strike.When index is less than the index strike price, the trader's sale price is buyer's price minus option premium.

The difficult part of a transaction such as this is finding a buyer willing to pay a premium over index to receive upside price protection. As many of the purchasing representatives at natural gas utilities are required to buy gas close to the index price corresponding to their specific supply locations, this form of structured pricing strategy probably won't entice them to proceed with such a transaction. However, if a trading company had sold Permian gas at $2.40, and the market subsequently fell to $2.15, it might be willing to enter into a purchase at a premium over index, still locking in a $2.30 cap for a $0.10 minimum margin.

Hedging and Trading Storage Capacity

This is one of the most interesting and potentially profitable structured transactions in the natural gas industry. If accurately evaluated and properly hedged, storage can provide a broad range of trading and service opportunities, whether it is used as an arbitrage vehicle, or as a tool for operational purposes.

The basic idea behind storage from an operational standpoint is that it provides flexibility for a pipeline, a producer, or an end user during periods of discrepancy between supply and demand. That is, during high and low demand cycles, these market participants can utilize storage capacity to smooth out the peaks and troughs in their supply and demand profiles. Hedging the costs of storage for these purposes is sometimes difficult, and to some market participants is viewed as a cost of doing business which can't always be avoided or minimized.

From a trading perspective, storage capacity can be utilized to protect against, or profit from, discrepancies between forecasted low demand cycles and high demand cycles, and the resulting price discrepancies between the two. The first example will illustrate how a trader can profit from a discrepancy between current prices and those in the future.

Suppose that during a particular month, a trader has an opportunity to sell 10,000 MMBtu/d of gas to an end user in the Houston Ship Channel (HSC) for the following month (30 days) at $2.00. After several unsuccessful attempts at buying gas for the next month at HSC below $2.00, the trader notices there is a $0.10 spread between prices for the remaining 10 days of the current month ($1.90) and the price its end user is willing to pay for gas the following month ($2.00). The trader decides to contact a storage company at HSC and obtain a quote for short-term storage capacity. The storage company provides the trader with the following cost structure:

Injection:	$0.025 / MMBtu
Withdrawal:	$0.025 / MMBtu
Carry:	$0.050 / MMBtu per month on average daily balance
Fuel:	included in injection and withdrawal fees

How does the trader evaluate whether or not it would be profitable to pay $1.90 for gas for the remaining 10 days of the current month, inject it into storage, carry it, withdraw it from storage, and sell it during the next month at $2.00? The first step is to calculate the carrying cost between the first injection day and the last withdrawal day. Since the storage company charges a carrying cost based on the average daily storage balance per month, the trader needs to calculate his average daily balance per month. This is the sum of the daily balances for each month, divided by the number of days in each month. Then, by applying the carrying cost ($0.05 / MMBtu) to each month's average daily balance, the trader can calculate his total carrying costs. In addition, the trader must calculate the total injection cost (total volume injected multiplied by the injection fee) and the total withdrawal cost (total volume withdrawn multiplied by the withdrawal fee). The simplest method for calculating these charges and illustrating the storage activity is to set up a spreadsheet which shows each day's activity for each month and the cumulative activity for that month. Table 5-1 is an example of what a simple spreadsheet for this transaction might look like.

Therefore, if the trader divides the total storage costs ($25,411) by the total sales volume (300,000 MMBtu), the trader can determine, on a per MMBtu basis, if the trade would be profitable. That is, $25,411 divided by 300,000 MMBtu equals $0.085 costs, versus a $0.10 positive month spread, results in a net profit of $0.015 per MMBtu, or $4,500 total profit on the trade. Therefore, the trader should pay $1.90 for 10,000 MMBtu/d for the remaining days of the current month, inject and store it in the storage facility, withdraw it the following month, and sell it to the end user at $2.00. Figure 5.7 illustrates this transaction. The schedule of payments and receipts which follows details the trader's cash flow and resultant profit on the trade.

Pay to HSC supplier - current month (−)	$1.90
Pay to storage (−)	$0.085
Receive from HSC market - next month (+)	$2.00
Total profit	$0.015 x 30
	contracts = $4,500

This example assumes the trader is not transporting the supply to and from the storage facility. In other words, the storage facility is located in both a production area and a market area. Although this is not truly a realistic assumption, buyers and sellers can provide transportation to and from the storage facility in specific instances. For example, an end user might have

Table 5-1

Storage Example #1

	Current Month	31 days		Next Month	30 days	
Day	**Inject Volume**	**Withdrawal Volume**	**Daily Balance**	**Day**	**Inject Volume**	**Withdrawal Volume**	**Daily Balance**

Day	Inject Volume	Withdrawal Volume	Daily Balance	Day	Inject Volume	Withdrawal Volume	Daily Balance
							300,000
1	0	0	0	1	0	-10,000	290,000
2	0	0	0	2	0	-10,000	280,000
3	0	0	0	3	0	-10,000	270,000
4	0	0	0	4	0	-10,000	260,000
5	0	0	0	5	0	-10,000	250,000
6	0	0	0	6	0	-10,000	240,000
7	0	0	0	7	0	-10,000	230,000
8	0	0	0	8	0	-10,000	220,000
9	0	0	0	9	0	-10,000	210,000
10	0	0	0	10	0	-10,000	200,000
11	0	0	0	11	0	-10,000	190,000
12	0	0	0	12	0	-10,000	180,000
13	0	0	0	13	0	-10,000	170,000
14	0	0	0	14	0	-10,000	160,000
15	0	0	0	15	0	-10,000	150,000
16	0	0	0	16	0	-10,000	140,000
17	0	0	0	17	0	-10,000	130,000
18	0	0	0	18	0	-10,000	120,000
19	0	0	0	19	0	-10,000	110,000
20	0	0	0	20	0	-10,000	100,000
21	0	0	0	21	0	-10,000	90,000
22	30,000	0	30,000	22	0	-10,000	80,000
23	30,000	0	60,000	23	0	-10,000	70,000
24	30,000	0	90,000	24	0	-10,000	60,000
25	30,000	0	120,000	25	0	-10,000	50,000
26	30,000	0	150,000	26	0	-10,000	40,000
27	30,000	0	180,000	27	0	-10,000	30,000
28	30,000	0	210,000	28	0	-10,000	20,000
29	30,000	0	240,000	29	0	-10,000	10,000
30	30,000	0	270,000	30	0	-10,000	0
31	30,000	0	300,000				

Total Inject / Withdrawal	300,000	0		0	-300,000	
Inject fee / Withdrawal fee	$0.025	$0.025		$0.025	$0.025	
Total Inject / Withdrawal Costs	$7,500	$0		$0	$7,500	

Average Daily Balance	53,226		155,000
Carrying fee	$0.050		$0.050
Total Carrying Costs	$2,661		$7,750

Total Storage Costs:

Inject / Withdrawal Current Month	7,500
Inject / Withdrawal Next Month	7,500
Carrying Costs Current Month	2,661
Carrying Costs Following Month	7,750
	$25,411

transportation capacity from a storage facility to its destination point, and would therefore be able to purchase storage supply at the outlet of the facility from the trader. In addition, a producer might have transportation capacity from its production area point to the storage facility and would therefore be able to sell gas to the trader at the inlet to the storage facility. However, in

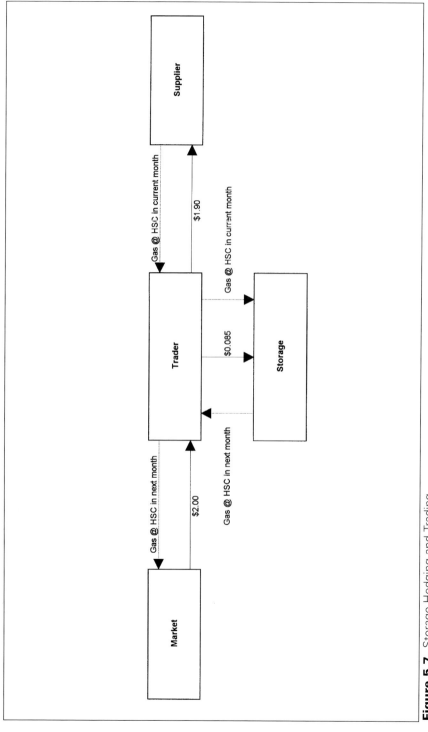

Figure 5.7. Storage Hedging and Trading

165

those instances where a trader is buying supply in a production area, transporting it to the storage facility, storing it, withdrawing it at a later date, transporting it to a market area, and selling it, the trader must allow for not only the transportation charges to and from the storage facility, but also for fuel loss from both the production area to the storage facility, as well as from the storage facility to the market area. In such a case, if the trader in the above example had to pay $0.05 / MMBtu to transport the supply to the storage facility, and $0.05 / MMBtu to transport the supply to the market area, the month spread ($0.10) would not have been large enough to cover the cost of transportation, let alone the added cost for lost supply due to fuel charges by the pipeline(s).

Here's a more complex storage example. Assume the trader in the previous example can obtain the same storage capacity arrangement from the same storage company.

Injection:	$0.025 / MMBtu
Withdrawal:	$0.025 / MMBtu
Carry:	$0.050 / MMBtu per month on average daily balance
Fuel:	included in injection and withdrawal fees

This time, however, we will assume the trader has to pay $0.05 / MMBtu (inclusive of surcharges) plus 2% fuel in-kind for transportation to the storage facility from the production area where he is buying supply (NGPL M.C.), and the same charge and fuel for transportation from the storage facility to the market area where he is selling the supply (Chicago city-gate). Assume the trader can pay a fixed price for gas at NGPL M.C. for any given month, and sell the supply to a market at Chicago c.g. index plus $0.02 for any given month. (Note: Assume transportation arbitrageurs have made it impossible to obtain transportation from NGPL M.C> to Chicago c.g. during the same month and make a profit.)

The first thing the trader needs to know are the costs he will incur bringing the gas to and from the storage facility. (Assume the trader can only sell a maximum of 10,000 MMBtu/d to the market at Chicago c.g. for any given month.) Therefore, if the trader transports gas to and from the storage facility, he will incur a $0.05 / MMBtu charge on both transportation legs for a total of $0.10 / MMBtu. In addition, because he wants to sell 10,000 MMBtu/d to the market at Chicago c.g., he will have to initially buy enough supply such that, after transportation in-kind fuel charges by the pipeline(s) both to and from the storage facility (storage fuel charges are included in the injection and withdrawal fees), the trader can deliver exactly 10,000 MMBtu/d to Chicago c.g. The easiest method of calculating the *netback* volume is to start at the end (delivered volume) and work backward to the beginning (received or purchased volume) by dividing each volume by the reciprocal of the fuel percentage. The following calculations illustrate this process:

Delivered Volume	÷	Reciprocal	=	Receipt Volume
10,000 MMBtu/d sale		.98		10,204 MMBtu/d at storage outlet
10,204 MMBtu/d at storage inlet		.98		10,412 MMBtu/d purchase

Therefore, the trader must buy an additional 412 MMBtu/d to allow for in-kind fuel charges both to and from the storage facility. The per MMBtu cost for this fuel is determined based on the cost of the supply. In other words, if the trader is going to pay $2.00 for 10,412 MMBtu/d for 30 days, but is only going to sell 10,000 MMBtu/d for 30 days, 412 MMBtu/d for 30 days (12,360 MMBtu) at $2.00, or $24,720, will be lost. Divide this amount by the total sale volume (10,000 MMBtu/d times 30 days equals 300,000 MMBtu), to see that the trader will incur an approximately $0.085 / MMBtu cost for fuel. If the trader pays $1.50 for the supply, the cost would represent $0.0625 / MMBtu, and if the trader pay $2.50 for the supply, the cost would represent $0.1025 / MMBtu. Assume the trader's purchase price is $2.00 for this example.

In addition to these costs of bringing the gas to and from the storage facility, and the costs of injecting and withdrawing the gas from storage, the trader will be paying carrying costs depending on how long the gas is stored. Assume the trader is injecting at the same rate (10,204 MMBtu/d) from the first through the 30th of the first month, and withdrawing at the same rate (10,204 MMBtu/d) from the first through the 30th of the month in which the sale occurs. Using the spreadsheet model from this example, we can determine the following carrying cost schedule (Table 5-2).

Inject one month, withdraw next	$0.0517 / MMBtu
Inject one month, carry one month, withdraw next	$0.1017 / MMBtu
Inject one month, carry two months, withdraw next	$0.1517 / MMBtu

The first scenario (inject one month, withdrawal the next) is slightly over the $0.05 / MMBtu carrying cost specified by the storage company. This is because of the average daily balance calculations for the injection month (155,000 MMBtu) and the withdrawal month (155,000 MMBtu). Together, the average daily balances total 310,000 MMBtu, which is different than if the storage capacity was 300,000 MMBtu from the beginning of the month to the end (in the case of storing for one month in between the injection month and the withdrawal month).

Here is a summary of the trader's comprehensive costs / MMBtu.

Transport to storage:	$0.05
Storage injection:	$0.025
Carry:	$0.052 (rounded)
Storage withdrawal:	$0.025
Transport to market:	$0.05
Transport fuel:	$0.085
Total costs	$0.287 + $0.05 for each additional month carry.

Table 5-2

				Storage Example #2				

| | | **Purchase Month** | **Sep** | | | **Sale Month** | **Nov** | |

Day	Inject Volume	Withdrawal Volume	Daily Balance	Day	Inject Volume	Withdrawal Volume	Daily Balance
							300,000
1	10,000	0	10,000	1	0	-10,000	290,000
2	10,000	0	20,000	2	0	-10,000	280,000
3	10,000	0	30,000	3	0	-10,000	270,000
4	10,000	0	40,000	4	0	-10,000	260,000
5	10,000	0	50,000	5	0	-10,000	250,000
6	10,000	0	60,000	6	0	-10,000	240,000
7	10,000	0	70,000	7	0	-10,000	230,000
8	10,000	0	80,000	8	0	-10,000	220,000
9	10,000	0	90,000	9	0	-10,000	210,000
10	10,000	0	100,000	10	0	-10,000	200,000
11	10,000	0	110,000	11	0	-10,000	190,000
12	10,000	0	120,000	12	0	-10,000	180,000
13	10,000	0	130,000	13	0	-10,000	170,000
14	10,000	0	140,000	14	0	-10,000	160,000
15	10,000	0	150,000	15	0	-10,000	150,000
16	10,000	0	160,000	16	0	-10,000	140,000
17	10,000	0	170,000	17	0	-10,000	130,000
18	10,000	0	180,000	18	0	-10,000	120,000
19	10,000	0	190,000	19	0	-10,000	110,000
20	10,000	0	200,000	20	0	-10,000	100,000
21	10,000	0	210,000	21	0	-10,000	90,000
22	10,000	0	220,000	22	0	-10,000	80,000
23	10,000	0	230,000	23	0	-10,000	70,000
24	10,000	0	240,000	24	0	-10,000	60,000
25	10,000	0	250,000	25	0	-10,000	50,000
26	10,000	0	260,000	26	0	-10,000	40,000
27	10,000	0	270,000	27	0	-10,000	30,000
28	10,000	0	280,000	28	0	-10,000	20,000
29	10,000	0	290,000	29	0	-10,000	10,000
30	10,000	0	300,000	30	0	-10,000	0

Total Inject / Withdrawal	300,000	0			0	-300,000	
Inject fee / Withdrawal fee	$0.025	$0.025			$0.025	$0.025	
Total Inject / Withdrawal Costs	$7,500	$0			$0	$7,500	

Average Daily Balance	155,000		155,000
Carrying fee	$0.050		$0.050
Total Carrying Costs	$22,750	includes $15,000 for Oct charge	$7,750

Total Storage Costs:

Inject / Withdrawal Current Month	7,500
Inject / Withdrawal Next Month	7,500
Carrying Costs for Sep	7,750
Carrying Costs for Oct	15,000
Carrying Costs for Nov	7,750
	$45,500
or	$0.152 per mmBtu

For the trader to profit from utilizing storage, the spread between what he can buy supply during one month and sell it for during the next month must be at least $0.287 to break even. If the trader is planning to carry the gas an additional month, the spread must be at least $0.337 to break even.

Suppose the trader has a opportunity to pay $2.00 for 10,412 MMBtu/d to a producer at NGPL M.C. for the month of September. The trader can sell 10,000 MMBtu/d to a market at Chicago c.g. at Chicago c.g. index plus $0.02 for any given month. How does the trader determine what the spread is between this fixed price and Chicago c.g. index plus $0.02 for October? The trader should calculate what the Chicago c.g. fixed-float index swap is by obtaining the bid for an October Chicago c.g. basis swap, and adjusting October futures by that differential, or obtaining a bid for the Chicago c.g. fixed-float index swap outright. If October Chicago c.g. basis swaps are L3D plus $0.01 bid, and October futures are $2.25 bid, the Chicago c.g. fixed-float index swap is therefore $2.26 bid, which would convert the trader's sale price to his market into $2.28. Even though the withdrawal month follows the injection month (no additional carry month), the $0.28 spread is not sufficient to cover the trader's costs ($0.287) and make a profit.

What about the spread from September NGPL M.C. ($2.00) to November Chicago c.g.? Assume that the November Chicago c.g. basis swap is also L3D plus $0.01 bid, but November futures are $2.35 bid. This implies a Chicago c.g. fixed-float index swap bid of $2.36, which converts the trader's sale price effectively into $2.38. Even with the additional $0.05 / MMBtu carrying cost charge, the $0.38 spread from the trader's September NGPL M.C. supply ($2.00) to his November Chicago c.g. market ($2.38) is sufficient to cover his costs of both storage and transportation ($0.337) and leave a $0.043 / MMBtu profit, or $12,900.

The trader should pay $2.00 for 10,412 MMBtu/d of NGPL M.C. supply from the producer, sell 30 November futures at $2.35, sell 10,000 MMBtu/d to his market at Chicago c.g. index plus $0.02, and sell one contract/d of a Chicago c.g. basis swap at L3D plus $0.01 to lock-in the $0.38 / MMBtu spread. The trader will then transport the 10,412 MMBtu/d of supply from the production region to the storage facility, and inject 10,204 MMBtu/d (after 2% fuel) into his storage capacity at the facility every day for the month of September where it will remain until November. During L3D November, the trader will buy back the futures he sold to lock in the month spread. Then, every day during the month of November, the trader will withdrawal 10,204 MMBtu/d of supply from the storage facility, transport it to Chicago c.g., and sell 10,000 MMBtu/d (after 2% fuel) to his market at November Chicago c.g. index plus $0.02. The transaction is complete. A schedule of payments and receipts which details the trader's cash flows and resulting profit follow.

Pay to NGPL M.C. supplier - Sep. (−)	$2.00
Futures sold (+)	$2.35
Futures bought at liquidation (−)	L3D
Receive from Chicago c.g. Basis swap (+)	L3D + $0.01
Pay to Chicago c.g. Basis swap (−)	Chicago c.g. index
Receive from Chicago c.g. market - Nov (+)	Chicago c.g. index + $0.02
Pay transport to storage (−)	$0.05
Pay to storage (−)	$0.152
Pay to transport from storage (−)	$0.05
Fuel in-kind charge (−)	$0.085
Total profit	$0.043 x 30 contracts
	= $12,900

A myriad of trading opportunities and operational strategies exist which can be implemented through the use of storage facilities. The examples here are only the basic trading strategies. It is up to the creativity of the trader and the expertise of other market participants to capitalize on the many possibilities for managing and trading storage capacity.

Buying Gas at a Floating Nearby Futures Price

Occasionally a seller may request a pricing structure based on (floats with) the nearby futures contract. For obvious reasons, this would be of greater benefit to a seller if the nearby futures price rises during the month than if the seller had simply sold at one fixed price for the duration of the month. Transactions such as these can be structured in several ways.

One method of pricing gas based on the nearby futures contract is to define the price received by the seller for a given month as the average of the daily futures settlement prices for the nearby contract during that given month. In other words, the averaging period will begin on the first day of the physical delivery month, using the settlement price of the nearby futures contract on that day as the first price in the average. If the first day of the month falls on a weekend, the settlement price of the nearby futures contract on Monday will either count as two days (if the first day of the month is a Sunday) or three days (if the first day of the month is a Saturday). Thereafter, the settlement price of the nearby futures contract on Fridays will count as three days (Friday, Saturday, and Sunday.), and the last trading day of the nearby futures contract will count as the remaining number of days in the physical delivery month. Since futures expire four (KCBT) or five (NYMEX) business days prior to the end of the month, the last trading day's settlement price is plugged into the monthly average for these days. Although this pricing method is somewhat complicated in addition to an accounting nightmare, it is used. Here is an example of how a trader can hedge such a transaction.

Suppose that on February 22nd, March futures have just expired and a seller proposes a transaction to a trader wherein the trader will pay the seller the average of all the April futures settlement prices (conforming to the specifications outlined previously), plus or minus some differential, during the month of March for gas delivered at PEPL OK the entire month of March. At what differential to April futures should the trader be willing to buy March PEPL OK gas, and how can the trader hedge this price risk? Assuming the trader can sell March PEPL OK gas at $2.00, Figure 5.8a will help illustrate the price risk the trader is exposed to.

As you can see, even though the supply price is based on the price of a different month, this is another form of fixed versus floating risk. The trader will receive a fixed price from her market for March PEPL OK, but will be paying a floating price to her supplier for March PEPL OK. The trader must, therefore, convert the fixed price received from the market into the same, or higher, floating price being paid to the supplier, or convert the floating price paid to the supplier into the same, or lower, fixed price received from the market. Although some trading firms will enter into a financial swap which can be tailored to match the floating price the trader will be paying to the supplier, assume the trader hedges the transaction without the use of a tailored swap. To hedge this transaction, therefore, the trader will need to buy April futures once the transaction is negotiated, and subsequently sell them throughout the month (March) at each of the daily April settlement prices to replicate the monthly average of all settlement prices of the April contract during March.

What differential to the April futures contract should the trader negotiate with the supplier? Since the trader can sell March PEPL OK at $2.00, it depends on the current price of April futures. If April futures are trading $2.25, the trader should negotiate a differential to April futures with the supplier that is wider than minus $0.25. In fact, because of the hedging risk and accounting complexities, the trader should be able to negotiate a differential which allows for at least a $0.05 profit margin. In this example, assume the trader successfully negotiates a minus $0.30 differential to the average of the settlement prices for the April futures contract as the price to be paid to the supplier.

Once the differential has been negotiated and agreed to, the trader should immediately pay $2.25 for 31 April futures contracts (31 days in March) to effectively convert the March PEPL OK sale at $2.00 into an April futures minus $0.25 price. Assume the trader is successful at selling back (liquidating) all of the April futures at the settlement prices corresponding to the settlement prices in the previously defined average paid to the supplier, the following diagram illustrates how this transaction would look once it has been hedged, and the schedule of payments and receipts which follows shows the trader's total profit.

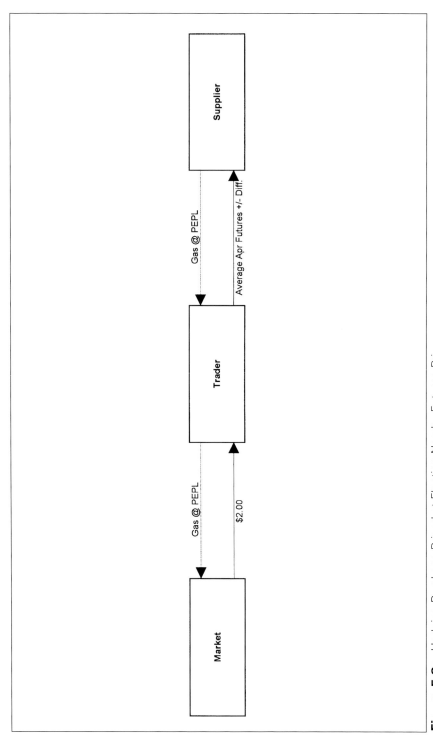

Figure 5.8a. Hedging Purchase Priced at Floating Nearby Futures Price

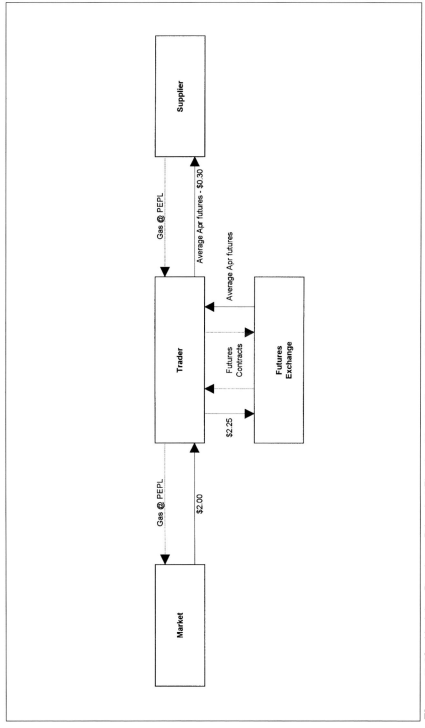

Figure 5.8b. Hedging Purchase Priced at Floating Nearby Futures Price

Receive from March PEPL OK market (+) $2.00
Futures bought - April (−) $2.25
Futures sold during March (+) Defined average
Pay to March PEPL OK supplier (−) Defined average - $0.30
Slippage due to missed settlements (−) $0.02

Total profit $0.03 x 31 contracts = $9,300

Although the pricing method in this example is sometimes used, the most common form of pricing for physical gas delivered in the current month based on the nearby futures contract is to structure the trade as a floating trigger. Using the example, once the trader and supplier have agreed on the differential to April futures for the March PEPL OK supply, the supplier is given the right to lock in, or trigger, the effective price it receives for its March PEPL OK up to the expiration of the April contract (five or six business days prior to the end of March). If the supplier does not trigger prior to the last half hour of trading on expiration day, the default price becomes the final day's settlement price adjusted for the differential. Let's assume the trader negotiates a minus $0.28 differential to April futures with the supplier for March PEPL OK supply, sells March PEPL OK gas at $2.00 to the market, and pays $2.25 for 31 April futures. Here are two extreme cases which show the trader's schedule of payments and receipts where the supplier defaults to the final day's settlement price as the trigger price.

Assume final day's settlement price is $2.75.

Receive from March PEPL OK market (+) $2.00
Futures bought - April (−) $2.25
Futures sold at April expiration (+) $2.75
Pay to March PEPL OK supplier (−) $2.47 ($2.75 − $0.28 = $2.47)

Total profit $0.03 x 31 contracts = $9,300

Assume final day's settlement price is $1.75.

Receive from March PEPL OK market (+) $2.00
Futures bought - April (−) $2.25
Futures sold at April expiration (+) $1.75
Pay to March PEPL OK supplier (−) $1.47 ($1.75 − $0.28 = $1.47)

Total profit $0.03 x 31 contracts = $9,300

The trader is hedged in both cases and captures a $9,300 profit no matter what the April futures price is at settlement. This is similar to an ordinary trigger structure with the added flexibility of pushing the default trigger date through the month to the expiration of the next nearby futures contract instead of the futures contract corresponding to the physical delivery month. In fact, if the trader and the supplier had originally entered into a normal trigger structure (trader buys March gas from supplier at a trigger differential to March futures), but the supplier wanted to roll the trigger into the new nearby contract, the trader could roll the existing March futures position from the original trigger into the April contract by selling 31 March futures and simultaneously buying 31 April futures. However, if there is a price difference between the March futures price and the April futures price at the time of the roll, the trigger differential would have to be adjusted by the same amount to maintain equality in pricing of the underlying gas. Furthermore, this rolling could continue for several months if the customer chose, however, because the trader would effectively be borrowing money (purchase price times quantity) from the customer by deferring payment, the customer should build in additional margin to the new differential each time the trigger is rolled to a new month.

Selling Gas at a Floating Nearby Futures Price

Occasionally a buyer may request a pricing structure based on the nearby futures contract. For obvious reasons, this would be of greater benefit to a buyer if the nearby futures price falls during the month than if the buyer had simply paid a single fixed price for the duration of the month. Transactions such as these can be structured in several ways.

One method of pricing gas based on the nearby futures contract is to define the price paid by the buyer for a given month as the average of the settled futures prices for the nearby contract during that given month. In other words, the averaging period will begin on the first day of the physical delivery month, using the settlement price of the nearby futures contract on that day as the first price in the average. Here is an example of how a trader can hedge such a transaction.

Suppose that on February 22nd, March futures have just expired and a buyer proposes a transaction to a trader wherein the buyer will pay the trader the average of all the daily April futures settlement prices, plus or minus some differential, during the month of March for gas delivered at PEPL OK the entire month of March. At what differential to April futures should the trader be willing to sell March PEPL OK gas, and how can the trader hedge this price risk? Assume the trader can pay $2.00 for March PEPL OK gas, and Figure 5.9a will help illustrate the price risk the trader is exposed to.

Even though the sale price is based on the price of a different month, this is another form of fixed versus floating risk. The trader will receive a floating price from the market for March PEPL OK, but will be paying a fixed price

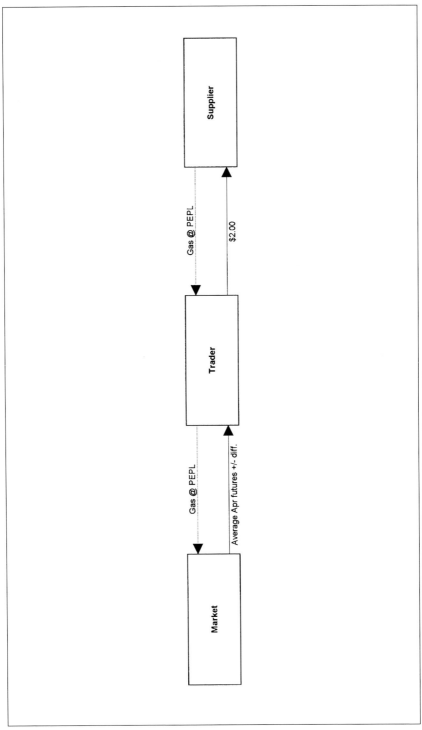

Figure 5.9a. Hedging Sale Priced at Floating Nearby Futures Price

to the supplier for March PEPL OK. The trader must, therefore, convert the fixed price paid to the supplier into the same, or lower, floating price the trader is receiving from market, or convert the floating price from the market into the same, or higher, fixed price being paid to the supplier.

Although some trading firms will enter into a financial swap which can be tailored to match the floating price the trader will receive from market, assume the trader hedges the transaction without the use of a tailored swap. To hedge this transaction, therefore, the trader will need to sell April futures once the transaction is negotiated, and subsequently buy them back throughout the month (March) at each of the April settlement prices to replicate the monthly average of all settlement prices of the April contract.

What differential to the April futures contract should the trader negotiate with the market? Since the trader can pay $2.00 for March PEPL OK, it depends on the current price of April futures. If April futures are trading $2.35, the trader should negotiate a differential to April futures with the market that is tighter than minus $0.35. In fact, because of the hedging risk and accounting difficulties, the trader should be able to negotiate a differential which allows for at least a $0.05 profit margin. In this example, assume the trader successfully negotiates a minus $0.30 differential to the average of the settlement prices for the April futures contract as the price from the market.

Once the differential has been negotiated and agreed to, the trader should immediately sell 31 April futures contracts (31 days in March) at $2.35 to effectively convert the $2.00 March PEPL OK purchase into an April futures minus $0.35 price. If we assume the trader is successful at buying back (liquidating) all the April futures at the daily April settlement prices during March corresponding to the settlement prices in the previously defined average pricing received from the market, this diagram will illustrate how this transaction would look once it has been hedged, and the schedule of payments and receipts which follows shows the trader's total profit.

Pay to March PEPL OK supplier (−)	$2.00
Futures sold - April (+)	$2.35
Receive from March PEPL OK market (+)	Defined average − $0.30
Futures bought during March (−)	Defined average
Slippage due to missed settlements (−)	$0.02
Total profit	$0.03 x 31 contracts = $9,300

Although the pricing method in this example is sometimes used, the most common form of pricing for physical gas delivered in the current month based on the nearby futures contract is to structure the trade as a floating trigger. Using this example, once the trader and market have agreed on the differential to April futures for the March PEPL OK supply, the market is given the right to lock-in, or trigger, the effective price it pays to the trader for March PEPL OK gas up to the expiration of the April contract (five or six business

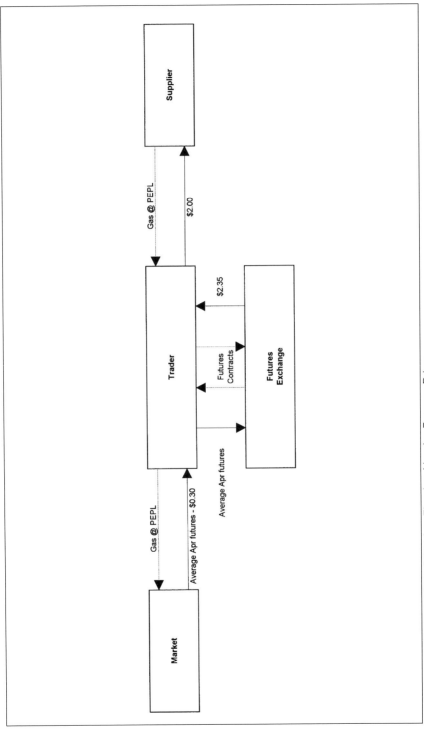

Figure 5.9b. Hedging Sale Priced at Floating Nearby Futures Price

178

days prior to the end of March). If the market does not trigger prior to the last half hour of trading on expiration day, the default price becomes the final day's settlement price adjusted for the differential. Assume the trader negotiates a minus $0.32 differential to April futures with market for March PEPL OK, pays $2.00 for March PEPL OK gas, and sells 31 April futures at $2.35. Here are two extreme cases which show the trader's schedule of payments and receipts where the market defaults to the final day's settlement price as the trigger price.

Assume final day's settlement price is $2.75.

Pay to March PEPL OK supplier (−)	$2.00
Futures sold - April (+)	$2.35
Futures bought at expiration - April (−)	$2.75
Receive from March PEPL OK market (+)	$2.43 ($2.75 − $0.32 = $2.43)

Total profit $0.03 x 31 contracts = $9,300

Assume final day's settlement price is $1.75.

Pay to March PEPL OK supplier (−)	$2.00
Futures sold - April (+)	$2.35
Futures bought at expiration - April (−)	$1.75
Receive from March PEPL OK market (+)	$1.43 ($1.75 − $0.32 = $1.43)

Total profit $0.03 x 31 contracts = $9,300

The trader is hedged in both cases and captures a $9,300 profit no matter what the April futures price is at settlement.

Paying a Premium Over Market to a Supplier and Making a Profit

This is a tricky way to pay a seller a large premium over index for gas and still make a net profit. The concept is to agree to pay the seller an above-market premium for gas in one month, contingent on being able to buy gas from that seller at a fixed price in a later month. This is effectively a short-term loan from the trader to the seller. This example will help clarify the mechanics of such a transaction.

Assume a trader obtains the following prices at a particular point in time for the markets listed next.

Month	Futures	Transco Zone 3 Basis Swap	Transco Zone 3 Index Gas
Nov.	$2.03	L3D + $0.01	Index + 0.01
Dec.	$2.10	L3D + $0.03	Index + 0.02
Jan.	$2.27	L3D + $0.05	Index + 0.03
Feb.	$2.16	L3D + $0.02	Index + 0.02
Mar.	$2.08	L3D + $0.01	Index + 0.01
Apr.	$1.99	L3D + $0.00	Index + 0.01

By combining these three prices for each month, the trader can obtain the implied Transco Zone 3 fixed prices for physical gas for each month.

Month	Transco Zone 3 Fixed Price
Nov.	$2.05
Dec.	$2.15
Jan.	$2.35
Feb.	$2.20
Mar.	$2.10
Apr.	$2.00

In addition, let's assume that the trader's cost of capital is 10% annually. Furthermore, let's assume the trader can sell physical gas at the index prices listed above for any month. For example, if the trader pays the supplier index plus $0.11 for 10,000 MMBtu/d of Nov. Transco Zone 3, and sells it at Nov. Transco Zone 3 index plus $0.01, he will lose $30,000 (i.e., 10,000 MMBtu/d times 30 days times $0.10 loss). In addition, the trader's company will forego interest on these lost funds until they can be recovered. What fixed price would the trader need to pay for February supply, for example, to make a net profit on the two transactions, after the cost of capital expense?

The trader can structure the Feb purchase in one of a number of combinations between volume and fixed price, such that the $30,000, plus the interest and a nice profit, can be recovered. For instance, the trader could bid the supplier $2.052 for 10,000 MMBtu/d of February Transco Zone 3 and earn a $0.04 / MMBtu profit. Or the trader could bid the supplier $2.088 for 15,000 MMBtu/d of supply and earn the same $0.04 / MMBtu profit.

Assume the trader pays November Transco Zone 3 index plus $0.11 to the supplier for 10,000 MMBtu/d of November physical gas and sells it to a market at November Transco Zone 3 Index plus $0.01, taking a $0.10 / MMBtu loss. In addition, assume the trader can pay $2.105 to the supplier for 20,000 MMBtu/d of Transco Zone 3 gas in February. For protection, the trader hedges this fixed-price risk by selling 56 February futures contracts at $2.16, hedges the basis risk by selling two contracts/d of February Transco Zone 3 basis swaps at L3D plus $0.02, and sells the physical gas at February Transco Zone 3 index plus $0.02. Figure 5.10 illustrates the transaction (assuming the futures contracts are successfully liquidated at L3D).

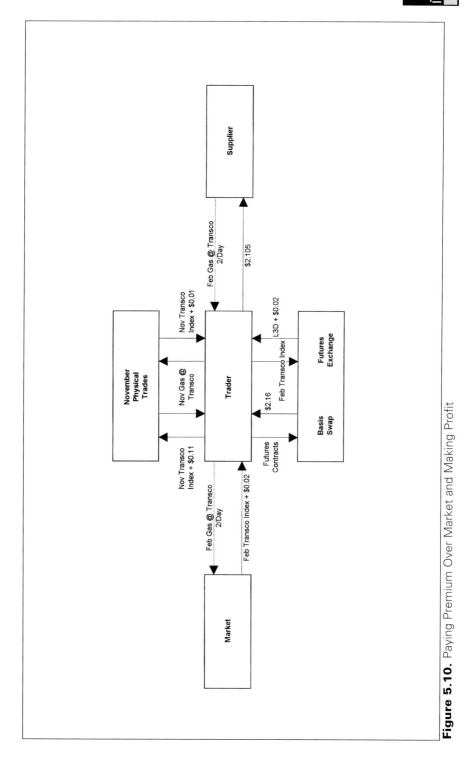

Figure 5.10. Paying Premium Over Market and Making Profit

Pay to supplier (−)	$2.105
Futures sold (+)	$2.16
Futures bought at expiration (−)	L3D
Receive from basis swap (+)	L3D + $0.02
Pay to basis swap (−)	Index
Receive from market (+)	Index + $0.02
Gross profit	$0.095 x 56 contracts = $53,200
Less cost of capital	($250)
Net profit	= $52,950

Transactions such as these are fairly rare. However, if there is extreme contango (prices in deferred months are at large premiums over first nearby month), and the seller is bearish on the specific deferred month in question, or if the seller can be convinced that the contango will soon disappear from the market curve, a trader can capitalize on this type of structured transaction.

Selling at a Discount to Market to a Buyer for a Profit

This is a tricky way to sell gas to a buyer at a deep discount to index and still make a net profit. The concept is to have the buyer agree to pay a below-market price for gas in one month, contingent upon being able to sell gas to that buyer at a fixed price in a later month. This is effectively a short-term loan by the trader to the buyer. The following example will help clarify the mechanics of such a transaction. Assume a trader obtains the following prices at a particular time for the markets listed below.

Month	Futures	Transco Zone 3 Basis Swap	Transco Zone 3 Index Gas
Nov.	$2.38	L3D + $0.01	Index + 0.01
Dec.	$2.25	L3D + $0.03	Index + 0.02
Jan.	$2.12	L3D + $0.05	Index + 0.03
Feb.	$1.96	L3D + $0.02	Index + 0.02
Mar.	$1.93	L3D + $0.01	Index + 0.01
Apr.	$1.89	L3D + $0.00	Index + 0.01

By combining these three prices for each month, the trader can obtain the implied Transco Zone 3 fixed prices for physical gas for each month.

Month	Transco Zone 3 Fixed Price
Nov.	$2.40
Dec.	$2.30
Jan.	$2.20
Feb.	$2.00
Mar.	$1.95
Apr.	$1.90

Assume the trader's cost of capital is 10% annually. Furthermore, let's assume the trader can buy physical gas at the index prices listed for any month. For example, if the trader sells 10,000 MMBtu/d to the buyer at index minus $0.08 for November Transco Zone 3, and buys it at November Transco Zone 3 index plus $0.02, he will lose $30,000 (i.e., 10,000 MMBtu/d times 30 days times $0.10 loss). In addition, the trader's company will forego interest on these lost funds until they can be recovered. At what fixed price would the trader need to sell gas in February, for example, in order to make a net profit on the two transactions, after the cost of capital expense?

The trader can structure the sale in one of a number of combinations between volume and fixed price, such that the $30,000, plus the interest and a nice profit, can be recovered. For instance, the trader could sell 10,000 MMBtu/d of February Transco Zone 3 to the buyer at $2.148 and earn a $0.04 / MMBtu profit (i.e., $30,250 / 280,000 MMBtu equals $0.108 loss, and $2.148 minus $2.00 equals $0.148 gain, resulting in $0.04 / MMBtu profit).

Assume the trader sells 10,000 MMBtu/d of November physical to the buyer at November Transco Zone 3 Index minus $0.08 and pays November Transco Zone 3 index plus $0.02 to a buyer for the same volume, taking a $0.10 / MMBtu loss. In addition, assume the buyer will pay $2.105 to the trader for 20,000 MMBtu/d of Transco Zone 3 gas in February. For protection, the trader hedges this fixed-price risk by paying $1.96 for 56 February futures contracts, hedges the basis risk by paying L3D plus $0.02 for two contracts/d of Feb Transco Zone 3 basis swaps, and pays February Transco Zone 3 Index plus $0.02 to a supplier for the physical gas. Figure 5.11 illustrates the transaction (assuming the futures contracts are successfully liquidated at L3D).

Receive from market (+)	$2.105
Futures bought (−)	$1.96
Futures sold at expiration (+)	L3D
Pay to basis swap (−)	L3D + $0.02
Receive from basis swap (+)	Index
Pay to supplier (−)	Index + $0.02
Gross profit	$0.105 x 56 contracts = $58,800
Less cost of capital	($250)
Net profit	= $58,550

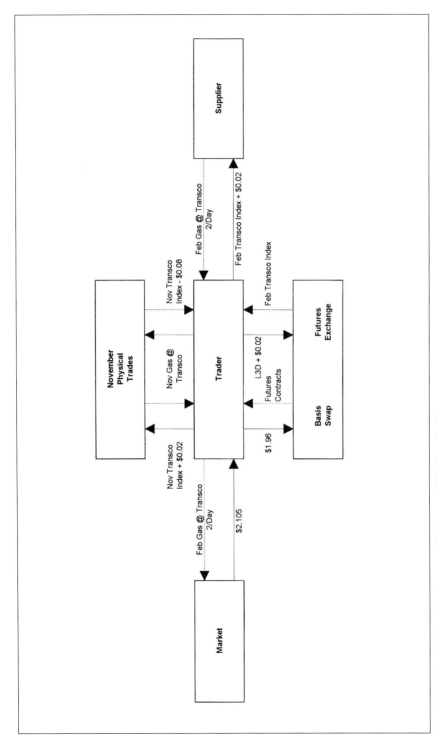

Figure 5.11. Selling Discount to Market and Making Profit

Transactions such as these are fairly rare. However, if there is extreme backwardation (prices in deferred months are at a deep discount to the first nearby month), and the buyer is bullish on the specific deferred month in question, or if the buyer can be convinced that the backwardation will soon disappear from the market curve, a trader can capitalize on this type of structured transaction.

Chapter 6

Building a Risk Management Model

This part of the text is intended to provide an idea of how to design a working model which brings together the various functions in a trading organization into a simple and efficient risk management structure. It should be noted that this chapter is merely a conceptual overview and will not cover detailed specifics, such as computer system requirements and system programming.

Centralized Risk Management

The importance of having a centralized risk management function cannot be emphasized enough, especially in larger trading organizations. Although there are several reasons why this is important, the four main purposes of the risk management function are to:

1. provide daily position reports to senior-level management which detail the organization's risks in all trading functions

2. Allow for efficient and accurate management of trading opportunities other than current-month cash transactions, and

3. Promote specialization among various business activities by breaking the activity into separately functioning and profit-oriented units.

4. Provide market information for decision-making

To begin, a successful natural gas trading organization should have the capability of performing the following basic trading functions: physical, futures and swaps, and transportation trading. Options trading, storage service, and financing services are some of the other functions which could be added to this model in a similar fashion. Each of the functions will have its own team of support personnel including systems, nominations/confirmations, and accounting.

The organization of these functions is really quite simple. Each function has what is called a *book*, essentially a record of all transactions which have

occurred or will occur, detailing the price, volume, counterparty, and tenure of each transaction. In addition, the book will be updated each time a transaction is entered to show new positions, if any, and the total profit or loss value of transactions. Transactions which are done for periods of time in the future are valued based on the price at which the transaction was executed versus the mid-market price each day. If physical gas for one year at some location is $2.00 bid, offered at $2.04 (mid-market equals $2.02), and a trader sells gas at that location at $2.04, the book will show, on that day, a $0.02 / MMBtu profit times the volume of the sale. If the trade creates an open short position, and on a subsequent day the mid-market price falls to $2.00 while that position is still open, the book will show a marked-to-market gain of an additional $0.02 / MMBtu for that day. The profit or loss of open positions will continue to fluctuate as long as the mid-market price is changing and until the position, or positions, are closed. It is up to the book manager to maintain the mid-markets for each market within the scope of the book.

The Fixed-Price Book

The *fixed-price book*, or futures book, is the simplest book to explain. Since, as of this writing, there are only three natural gas futures contracts (KCBT, Waha; NYMEX, Henry Hub; and NYMEX, Permian Basin), the fixed-price book has only three markets, or price curves, in it. However, even though futures contracts are traded out 18 months on each exchange, both markets can have as many as 15 years of pricing data. In other words, the fixed-price book must also contain fixed-float futures swaps for each exchange. Therefore, as futures and or futures swaps are traded, the book manager, will enter the trades by exchange, month, price, and number of contracts into the fixed-price book. The mid-market futures prices for each of the listed months are the settlement prices calculated by the exchange(s) after the close of trading each day. The mid-market prices for months or years beyond those listed by the exchange are calculated by the book manager according to month spreads and calendar spreads which reference the listed months. These spreads are traded in the OTC market, and the OTC futures swap brokers provide end-of-day bid/offer prices for these spreads which the book manager can use to determine and set the mid-markets for those deferred months and years each day. At the beginning and end of each day, therefore, the book manager can provide a list of all executed trades for the previous or current day, the profit or loss on those trades for that given day, the beginning and ending open position(s) of the book, and the marked-to-market and closed profit and loss of the entire book. Closed profit and/or loss is calculated as that amount which is realized after a position or positions have been closed.

The physical trading function is by far the most complicated unit in the model. As such, there are several books which can be formed to break down the components of a physical transaction so that each risk can be managed separately. Because natural gas is traded in so many different regions around North America, it is common for trading organizations to create regional desks to cover each specific region. A physical transaction at a fixed price is actually a physical transaction at index, combined with a basis swap, and a futures swap. In addition, if the physical transaction is occurring between two different locations, there is a transportation element involved as well. Stemming from these relationships, each regional desk should include an index book, a basis book, and a transport book. Therefore, each time a physical transaction, other than day-to-day transactions, is executed at the desk, the trade should be broken up into its component parts, and each of these parts should be entered into their respective books.

The Index Book

The index book is essentially a record of all physical trades and the resulting positions and profit or loss on those trades for a particular desk. More specifically, the index book is only concerned with the location, the volume, and the effective index price of physical transactions. Depending on the number of pipelines covered by a specific trading desk and the number of trading locations on each of those pipelines, the index book for a regional desk will contain many different markets, and many different tenures for each of those markets. In other words, the index book must contain every physical position, open or closed, taken by its corresponding desk on the pipelines and at each location which has been assigned to that specific desk. As a result, the index book for a particular desk might contain as many as 15 different pipelines, each having one or more locations at which physical gas is actively traded by that desk. It is up to the index book manager at each desk to make sure executed trades are entered at the correct price, under the correct pipeline, location, and for the correct tenure. In addition, the index book manager at each desk is responsible for maintaining accurate mid-market index prices at each location on each pipeline assigned to that desk. For example, if the index book manager is index flat bid, offered at index plus $0.02 at a particular region for physical gas for a three month term, the book manager should mark the index price curve at index plus $0.01 for those months.

The Basis Book

Similar to the index book, the basis book is essentially a record of all basis swap trades and the resulting positions and profit or loss on those trades for a particular desk. More specifically, the basis book is only concerned with the specific index in the basis swap, the volume (number of contracts), and the effective differentials of the basis swap transactions. Depending on the number of indexes reflecting pipelines covered by a specific trading desk

and the number of index locations on each of those pipelines, the basis book for a regional desk will contain many different markets and many different tenures for each of those markets. The basis book must contain every basis swap position, open or closed, taken by its corresponding desk on the pipeline indexes and at each index location on those pipelines which has been assigned to that specific desk. As a result, the basis book for a particular desk might contain as many as 15 different pipelines, each having one or more locations at which physical gas is actively traded by that desk. It is up to the basis book manager at each desk to make sure that executed basis trades are entered at the correct basis differential, under the correct index, and for the correct tenure. In addition, the basis book manager at each desk is responsible for maintaining accurate mid-market basis differentials for each index on each pipeline assigned to that desk.

The Transport Book

Like the index and basis books, the transport book is essentially a record of all executed transportation trades and the resulting positions and profit or loss on those trades for a particular desk. More specifically, the transport book is only concerned with the specific pipeline where the transportation capacity was obtained, the volume of capacity, and the effective transportation rate for the transactions. Depending on the number of pipelines covered by a specific trading desk, the transport book for a regional desk will contain many different pipelines and many different tenures for each of those pipelines, such as month-to-month capacity or long-term capacity. In other words, the transport book must contain every transportation position, open or closed, taken by its corresponding desk on the pipelines which have been assigned to that specific desk. As a result, the transport book for a particular desk might contain as many as 15 different pipelines, each having one or more tenures for which transportation capacity has been traded by that desk. It is up to the transport book manager at each desk to make sure that executed transportation capacity trades are entered at the correct rate, on the correct pipeline, for the correct volume, and for the correct tenure. In addition, the transport book manager at each desk is responsible for maintaining accurate mid-market transportation rates for each pipeline assigned to that desk for short- and long-term tenures. Bid and offer spreads are becoming more and more available via electronic bulletin boards whereby sellers of transportation capacity post an offer price and buyers post a bid price for various segments, volumes, and tenures of firm capacity. Since interruptible transportation rates are negotiated by the marketing representatives at the pipelines on a case-by-case basis, there is no way to accurately track the mid-market value of these rates. Therefore, the transport book manager is only obligated to maintain accurate mid-markets for firm capacity in the forward months.

Organization of Regional Desks

There are several functions at a regional desk, each of which should be performed by different individuals:

a. short-term physical traders (one month out or less),
b. mid-term physical traders (one month to one year out),
c. long-term physical traders (more than one year out),
d. financial trader (hedges risk in transactions),
e. nominations/confirmations, and
f. accounting.

In addition, each regional desk should have one person responsible for managing the desks macro decisions such as when to buy or sell, how much, and at what prices. To function most efficiently, it is important that all of the people at the desk be physically situated in close proximity to one another. The importance of this is evident, for example, in situations where a short-term trader's customer wants to extend a deal from the next day, for a term of three months. The short-term trader would ask the mid-term trader for a price quote for that duration and relay that quote to the customer. If the customer accepts the deal, the short-term trader writes up the details of the trade and provides one copy to the nominations/confirmations personnel and one copy to the accounting personnel.

Because each person at the desk is specializing in one function, required quotes for any specific opportunity from any member of the desk should be readily available and highly competitive. This type of a system works much better than one where each trader is trying to piece together various types of transactions on their own. For example, if the short-term trader is requested by a customer for a long-term quote, he or she doesn't need to make any phone calls during the day to keep track of the long-term markets, but instead can obtain that quote instantaneously from the long-term trader. In addition, if the trading functions at the desk are specialized according to pipelines and transaction tenures, the desk will avoid being arbitraged in these different markets by other market participants.

In some instances, companies are set up with different individual buyers and sellers within their companies, and it is not uncommon for one trader at the desk to try to buy gas from these firms and another trader at the desk to try to sell gas to the same firm at the same time. This scenario is obviously acceptable if the two traders can arbitrage the other company, but this rarely happens. The solution is to assign each desk trader to different companies to avoid overlap coverage. In general, however, it is extremely important for all traders at the desk to openly communicate potential trades before closing them.

Due to the nature of the natural gas pipeline network, many pipelines span from one region to another and possibly several others. Because of this, the different regional desks can often buy and sell with each other if they can transact at a better price than the market in each corresponding region. For example, suppose the mid-continent desk is long and the Northeast desk is short. Assume that transportation from the mid-continent to the Northeast is $0.25 / MMBtu, inclusive of all surcharges and fuel. If buyers in the mid-continent are only willing to pay $2.00, and sellers in the Northeast will only sell at $2.27, the two desks should transact with each other. The Northeast desk would pay the mid-continent desk $2.01, pay a transportation charge of $0.25 / MMBtu, and cover its short position at a net cost of $2.26. Each desk has benefited by $0.01 / MMBtu, and the company as a whole has benefited by $0.02 / MMBtu. It should be the responsibility of the desk managers to be aware of and continuously evaluate these potential opportunities.

The role of the financial trader for a particular desk is to execute all EFPs, trigger, and other differential pricing products, as well as hedge any fixed-price risk for the desk by transacting with the other books in the risk management model. For example, if a long-term trader at the desk is requested by a producer to bid for an EFP in the Permian for one year, the financial trader would be responsible for providing the long-term trader with a competitive differential quote. The financial trader would also be responsible for providing basis swap, swing swap, futures swap, and index gas quotes, as well as managing each of these books for the desk, with the exception of the fixed-price book.

In addition to managing and providing quotes for EFPs, basis swaps, and swing swaps, the financial trader must also manage the index book for his or her desk. That is, the financial trader manages the physical positions for the desk at each major trading point in the region assigned to that desk. It is the responsibility of the financial trader to maintain the index mid-markets for each trading point on each pipeline where the desk actively trades physical gas. As such, the financial trader provides quotes for index gas when they are requested by the other desk traders (Fig. 6.1).

Sample Transaction

Let's suppose that a trading company has an opportunity to sell 10,000 MMBtu/d of gas at a fixed price to a major natural gas utility on PEPL in Oklahoma for one year beginning the following month. How does the long-term trader arrive at the fixed-price to offer the utility? It should be the responsibility of the financial trader for the mid-continent desk.

Since the potential transaction is a physical sale at a fixed price at a location other than a futures contract delivery point, the financial trader will need prices for the following components to make a fixed-price offer for physical gas on PEPL in Oklahoma :

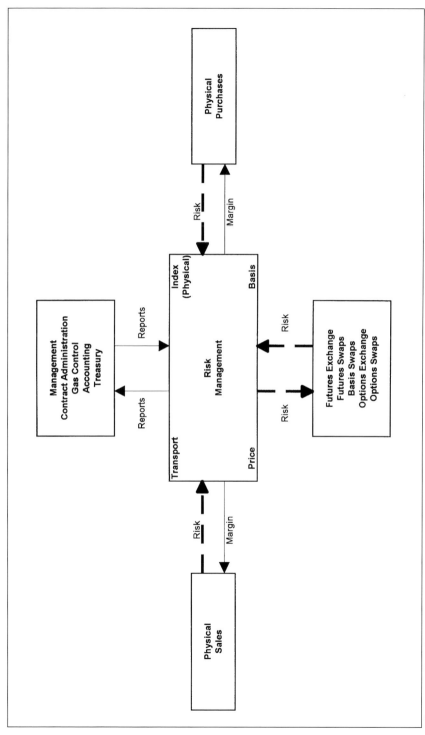

Fig. 6.1. The financial trader provides quotes for index gas when requested by other traders and regional desks.

1. fixed-float futures swap 1 year offer for 1 contract/d,
2. PEPL OK basis swap 1 year offer for 1 contract/d, and
3. PEPL OK index gas 1 year offer for 1 contract/d.

Since the mid-continent financial trader is not responsible for managing the fixed-price book, he must obtain the futures swap quote from the fixed-price book trader. To obtain the quotes for PEPL OK basis and index gas, the mid-continent financial trader uses his offers which are set in the respective books. Assume the mid-continent financial trader has index plus $0.025 set as the offer for one year physical PEPL OK index gas. Furthermore, assume the trader has L3D minus $0.25 set as the PEPL OK one year basis swap offer. Therefore, after obtaining a one year futures swap offer from the fixed-price book of $2.00, the mid-continent financial trader can calculate and relay a fixed-price offer to the long-term mid-continent trader as follows.

Futures swap offer	$2.00
Basis swap offer	L3D – $0.25
Index gas offer	index + $0.025
Fixed price offer	$2.00 – $0.25 + $0.025 = $1.775

The anticipated profit (difference between the offer prices and the mid-market prices) on the sale is $0.05 / MMBtu. Upon receiving $1.775 as a fixed-price offer for one year physical gas on PEPL in Oklahoma from the financial trader, the long-term trader submits a proposal to sell gas to the market at this price. If we assume the market accepts the offer, the long-term trader should be credited with 25% of the difference between the sale price and the mid-market price. This is only a suggested method of origination crediting. The remaining $0.0375 of margin will be divided equally between the various books to allow for some slippage in execution risk. Each book may be credited with more or less profit than its allocated residual (after origination credit to the long-term sales trader) depending on whether or not the book manager can cover the short position it will be left with as a result of making the sale. If, as a result of making the sale, a book manager closes a preexisting long position, the residual margin which was allocated to the book can be realized immediately. Otherwise, the allocated margin will be categorized as market-to-market profit (which is subject to increase or decrease depending on changes in market prices after the position has been created) until the position is closed.

Once the sale to the market has been made at $1.775 and the long-term trader has been credited with $0.0125 of origination profit, the following positions would be generated.

Fixed-price book	Short 1 year futures swap at $1.985 + $0.0125
Basis book	Short 1 year PEPL OK basis swap at – $0.275 + $0.0125
Index book	Short 1 year PEPL OK index gas at Index + $0.015 + $0.0125

Each book would be given a short position at its respective mid-market price plus its share of the allocated residual margin. Assuming the sale to the customer generated short positions in each book, the book managers would administer the new positions.

Although highly discretionary, the book managers in this example might try covering their open positions by attempting to pay mid-market or less for their swaps, futures, or index gas to capture (realize) all of the residual margin which has been allocated to them. For instance, if another long-term trader subsequently requested a bid to a supplier for one-year supply at the same point (PEPL OK) for the same term, the book traders might each provide their mid-market prices as their bids, instead of below mid-market bids, so that the long-term trader might have a better chance in closing the deal with the supplier. If this proved to be the case, and the trader was successful in procuring the supply for the price indicated, the book managers would not be required to do any trades as the purchase from the supplier would naturally cover the pre-existing short positions in each book from the earlier sale. If a trader completes a transaction with a customer which closes a position or positions in one or more of the books, the trader might be credited with closing credit instead of origination credit. This might be set by the book managers on a deal-by-deal basis in order to provide extra incentive to the traders in helping to close out existing positions. Alternatively, the trader could build his or her margin in the price before quoting it to the customer.

Conclusion

Trading natural gas as a career is more fun than I ever thought I'd have in my adult professional working life. What is most fun and satisfying to me, and probably to other traders in other markets, is applying my trading experience and testing my knowledge of various trading tools and trading techniques every day. I still learn something new every day about either myself, the market, or both. It's like a game that traders play to see who can do better than the others, as measured by our profit or loss at the end of the day. Obviously the game is more fun when the day is profitable, but it's almost as much fun to bounce back from a losing day and learn from the mistakes.

From changes in fundamental forces (weather patterns, pipeline, production, nuclear unit outages, or storage buying and selling) to technical developments (broken trendlines, closes above long-term moving averages, and key reversals), the natural gas market is a constant challenge. There is a certain thrill about formulating an idea for a trade, executing that trade, and watching it unfold exactly as it was originally envisioned. There's really nothing like it!

This book is an attempt to share some of the experience and knowledge of the trading tools and techniques unique to the natural gas market with those who would like to learn more about these ideas either to move into the trading side of the business or to truly understand exactly how and why they work. It may be helpful when a trader is conceptually sure of how to hedge a particular trade or optimize a specific trading opportunity, but is not completely comfortable with the mechanics of a certain instrument to be used or the math behind the pricing of a particular deal. In many instances, possibly, this book will be a starting point for more creative trading ideas and trading tools that have yet to be discovered.

There have been concerns expressed that I might be "selling industry secrets" in some regard, but I look at it as an investment. That is, the more that people in the market know the available tools and trading techniques, the more they will see their benefit and utilize them . As a result, the market will be more active for the rest of us. And, as everyone should know, the more active a market is and the more each type of player is represented, the more fairly it will reflect the value of what is being traded.

Although it is one of the smaller markets traded in terms of the total dollar amount of goods transacted, the natural gas market is gaining momentum and popularity. From its "environmentally correct" attributes to its widespread use as a source of power generation in a newly deregulated market for electricity, natural gas is gaining more respect than as just the byproduct it was once considered to be. Just since 1991 because of the volatility in the price of natural gas, many market participants are becoming more aware of the need for managing their price risk, which has given rise to a very active

financial derivative market for natural gas. Both the physical and financial markets for natural gas will continue to expand as more market participants, national and international (i.e., Canadian and Mexican), discover the benefits of natural gas and the need for price risk management.

I wish you the best of luck in your trading endeavors and hope to trade with you soon in the natural gas market.

Index

G

H